D1434196

Challenging and enlightening

Standing up for Christ in our post Christian society can feel difficult and demanding. Clare's book introduces us to women who sought to apply the Bible to their lives in a culture that had neglected God's word for generations. These sixteenth-century women who were married to leading reformers began to work out what it meant for them to trust Scripture alone, faith alone, grace alone and Christ alone for God's glory. We have inherited much from the faithfulness of Christians at that time but we, too, are tempted to neglect God's word and live by the values of our society. Reading the stories of these women not only brings the Reformation alive but it also exhorts us to be similarly grounded in God's Word. This is a great book for individual reading, book groups or even to study on a women's weekend away — it is both challenging and enlightening.

Karen Soole, Northern Women's Convention

I couldn't stop reading!

I couldn't stop reading about these six women!

I loved their passion to read the Bible when they were allowed to read it for themselves for the first time. Some had to wait while their husbands translated it for them!

They were scorned in society for marrying priests and all around them was persecution, controversy, plague and death yet they showed hospitality in a way that blew my mind.

Some were quiet and some outspoken but Jesus used them to change their world. They changed mine, too.

Liz Cox, St Giles' Church of England

I absolutely loved First Wives' Club

I absolutely loved First Wives' Club — *couldn't put it down!*

This book, beautifully written, was a joy to read. It gives us the portraits of six women who lived in the most dangerous but exciting time in history from a Christian point of view.

Their relationship to the Reformers gives the human interest to the book, but they were courageous, godly women in their own right, whom God was able to use in a complementary way in the recovery of the true gospel of Christ and its progress in Europe.

Great role models for today!

Christine Gobbett, Highbury Baptist Church

Highly recommended!

If, like me, you hated history at school, and know precious little about the Reformation, have no fear!

I found First Wives' Club *a great way to spend time with 6 very different Christian women who lived in the early 16th century, and to learn about the Reformation through their lives, marriages and home situations.*

Some showed great godliness and courage in the public arena of church politics alongside their husbands, others served quietly behind the scenes, giving generous hospitality and compassionate care; some were exemplary in their Christian life and witness, others were far from being ministry models!

Each biography is followed by a short suggested Bible passage and questions for study and reflection, which will help the reader to view the Wives, lives through 'Bible eyes' and see the challenges for their own life and faith. Highly recommended!

Christa Moll, St George's Church, Wembdon

I loved reading this book!

In First Wives' Club, *Clare Heath-Whyte writes about the lives of 6 sixteenth-century wives who lived in Europe during the Reformation. Each woman's experience of marriage and family life was different. Each of the women experienced different hardships and tragedies. But each sought to live their lives according to the Bible's teaching rather than the culturally acceptable practices of the day.*

Some of the women Clare writes about are well known; some I hadn't heard of before reading this book. A couple were exceptionally gifted; most were ordinary. Each enhanced their husband's effectiveness for the gospel by their support and sacrifice. Each has something to teach Christian women today about how to live whole-heartedly for Jesus in a culture that is increasingly hostile to Him.

Clare portrays each character warmly and with appreciation for their strengths and struggles. Her love of history and sense of humour is evident in each account. She is honest about the failings of the wives and their husbands — some of the details she records are shocking! She challenges the reader to be obedient to God's word in their own lives and provides helpful Bible study questions that encourage further reflection on the issues raised in each chapter.

Sixteenth-century Europe was not an easy place to live as a follower of Christ. The Reformers and their wives faced much hostility, and at times danger, as they believed and taught that the Bible was the authority by which Christians were to live and not the traditions of the church. This book will certainly inspire readers to stand firm in their faith and to maintain a gospel focus in each area of their lives. I loved reading this book and recommend it as a valuable resource for personal encouragement or group study.

Carolyn Lacey, author and speaker based in Worcester

First Wives' Club

Clare Heath-Whyte

First Wives' Club first published 2014 by 10Publishing

Copyright © 2014 by Clare Heath-Whyte
and 10Publishing
Reprinted 2016

ISBN: 978-1-909611-76-4

Designed by Diane Bainbridge

Printed and bound by CPI Group (UK) Ltd, Croydon,
CR0 4YY, England

10Publishing, a division of 10ofthose.com
Unit C Tomlinson Road, Leyland, PR25 2DY,
England

Email: info@10ofthose.com
Website: www.10ofthose.com

For my parents

CONTENTS

ACKNOWLEDGEMENTS

With grateful thanks:

To all at the Proclamation Trust Spring Wives' Conference who have given me the opportunity to spend time finding out about these women;

To Jonathan and all at 10ofthose.com for doing such a great job and for letting me write another book;

To Peter Newman Brooks, who first inspired me to look into Reformation family life;

To Sian, Vaughan and my parents for reading the manuscript and for giving me thoroughly biased familial encouragement;

To David, Katie and George for all their support and for appearing to be vaguely interested most of the time;

To David (again) who, in the words of Katharina Zell, 'granted and allowed me space and will to read, hear, pray, study ... even when it meant less attention to or neglect in looking after his physical needs and running his household'.[1]

INTRODUCTION

I wonder how you feel about reading the stories of women who lived and died 500 years ago – that's half a millennium! It all sounds a bit dull and dusty – all thees and thous – as well as old fashioned and irrelevant. After all, the world we live in is a very different place. In the twenty-first century we expect life to be fast paced and technological. The sepia-tinted past can't really have much to say to us today, can it? Even the world of my grandparents' youth seems incredibly distant – cars and planes were a novelty. We live in a time of great change. My parents can remember the excitement of seeing TV for the first time; when I was a child *colour* TV arrived; our children have never known a time without twenty-four-hour, multi-channel television – which can now be watched on a phone. We expect change. We expect new fashions in the shops season by season and every new gadget to be superseded in a matter of months.

How can looking back to the past help us in any way when so much has changed? Some changes are exciting. Others are unsettling. For all of us in the twenty-first century change is an incontrovertible fact of life – which can make life hard for us as Christians. When everything past generations took for granted is up for grabs, how can we be sure which way to turn? When we face hostility for standing up for truths, which until recently were generally accepted, what do we do? How can finding about a load of women who lived 500 years ago, at the time of the Reformation, help us to live for Christ in the challenging and confusing world of today?

In many ways the sixteenth century might seem very alien. Tudor England might be familiar from costume dramas and bestselling historical fiction, but the old-fashioned language, elaborate clothes and court rituals don't seem immediately relevant to the way we live today. During that same period mainland Europe, where all of these women lived, can feel even more distant to us now. The European countries we are familiar with were a long way in the future. Germany and Italy were then patchworks of princedoms and city states. Latin rather than English was the international language – the language of the super powerful Roman Catholic Church, as well as of classical Rome, which many of the educated elite understood better than their own time. In Europe today church-going is a minority activity, and theological debate seen as a bizarre irrelevance. 500 years ago everyone went to church, and theological differences not only divided families but also led to bitter wars. In many ways the sixteenth century was *very* different to the twenty-first.

In some ways, though, it was not so different. The 1500s were years of enormous change too. Technology was changing the way people communicated. We have Twitter; they had the printing press, enabling new ideas to be spread to a mass audience rather than each book having to be painstakingly copied by hand. Like today new ideas were challenging age-old beliefs. For centuries the Roman Catholic Church had dominated virtually all aspects of life. Yet increasingly people were criticising not only the immorality and greed of the clergy but also the key doctrines of the church. The certainties of the past were being questioned, rejected and replaced by new and radical ways of thinking and acting.

The most important question in an age of early and often sudden death – namely, how to enter heaven – now had a new answer. One's eternal destiny no longer rested on obedience to church teaching, performing certain good deeds and religious duties, and persuading relatives or paying others to pray for your soul. According to reformers such as Martin Luther salvation was a gift from God, bought at the price of His Son's death on the cross. The implications of this simple biblical idea were revolutionary. There was no longer any need for a priest to celebrate the Mass on behalf of the people – everyone could have direct access to God through Christ's once-for-all death on the cross. Priests or pastors did not have a hotline to God – He was available to all. Pastors were to teach

God's people, but *every* Christian had a valuable role to play in the church. Old values and assumptions were swept away. The Bible, and not church teaching, was to be the authority on how to please God. Compulsory celibacy for pastors and the superiority of the monastic life were questioned. Ordinary people were encouraged to read the Bible for themselves and to serve God in their everyday lives.

It was an exciting but terrifying time for many. Dealing with hostility and official opposition for standing up for biblical teaching is nothing new. Those who initially accepted the new teaching faced misunderstanding at best, death at worst. As time went by and the Reformation became established in some areas, the danger of military and political pressure from Catholic powers increased. To the ordinary sixteenth- (and twenty-first-) century anxieties of money, relationships, family and health were added persecution, insecurity and war.

Women also faced another familiar challenge. What did it look like to be a godly woman? How far were traditional models and attitudes applicable to a new generation? The challenge to live by the Bible rather than by following tradition or contemporary culture was the same for them as it is for us.

Unlike us these women had to work out what biblical womanhood looked like from scratch. There was no older generation of godly women to provide wisdom and advice on being a Christian wife and mother – the assumption had been that becoming a nun was a woman's high road to holiness. These Reformation women were pioneers, striving to put the Bible's teaching into practice in their own particular times and circumstances. They were the 'First Wives' Club' – the first generation of Christian women probably since apostolic times to seek to put the Bible into practice in marriage and family life. They were different women, with different husbands and family circumstances, with different personalities and gifts – Katie Luther was a wife, mother and businesswoman; Katharina Zell was a church worker alongside her husband; Argula von Grumbach was a writer, who used her gifts to defend the gospel; Wibrandis Rosenblatt – the wife of no less than four reformers! – was a caring companion and mother to a blended family; Anna Zwingli, living in difficult and dangerous times, had to deal with devastating bereavement; Idelette Calvin suffered ill health and a less than perfect marriage. Each of these women knew, or at least knew of, the others, and formed a network of friendship and support.

They each sought to apply the Bible's teaching to their own particular situation – with much success, some controversy and a few failures. In a changing and confusing world they found that the only solid foundation was living a life built, as the reformers would have put it, on Scripture alone, by faith alone, by grace alone, through Christ alone, giving God alone the glory.[1] We won't go far wrong if we follow their example today!

Clare Heath-Whyte

CHAPTER ONE

Katie Luther
1499–1552
A Life-Long Learner

As time goes by it gets harder to break old habits. Even as Christians it's easy to excuse ungodly behaviour because 'that's just what I'm like – I was born that way'. Whether it's a bad temper or a sharp tongue, extravagance or negativity, we can become so used to our unchrist-like personality traits that we don't even expect to change. As a young woman Katie Luther was known to be difficult and bossy and was determined to get her own way; by her death she was revered as a model of Protestant piety. She was still feisty, hardworking and stubborn, but these qualities had been harnessed to serve Christ and His people. As she studied God's Word she allowed the sword of the Spirit to do its painful work — changing and moulding her to reflect God's likeness.

In 1525 in Wittenberg, Germany, Katharina von Bora married Martin Luther, the man who had stood alone to challenge the teachings of the Roman Catholic Church, and so had launched what we now know as the Protestant Reformation. Luther was one of the most famous, and infamous, men of his generation. He was adored by those who had accepted his teaching — those who had been set free from ritual and legalism to enjoy a relationship with Christ on the basis of God's grace alone. He was loathed by those who felt he was destroying the basis of Christian civilisation by attacking Roman Catholic doctrine. He was also a monk who had made a vow of celibacy. Whoever married Martin Luther was going to be thrown into the limelight. During her twenty-one years of marriage Katie[1] would find herself copied and despised in equal measure as she tried to show that it was possible to please God as a married woman fully involved with the world around her.

That might seem obvious to us, but in the early sixteenth century women who wanted to please God were expected to join a convent, make vows of chastity, poverty and obedience, and renounce the world. In fact that was exactly what Katie herself had done – although not entirely voluntarily. She had been packed off to a Benedictine convent when she was just five years old after her father's remarriage. That meant the family had one less mouth to feed and no dowry to pay in the future. She moved to a Cistercian cloister when she was nine, where a relative was the abbess and her Aunt Lena also lived. When she was fifteen, on 8 October 1515, Katie took her vows and became a nun. Life in a convent was not as grim as we might expect. In an age when there were few opportunities for women to be educated, Katie learnt to read and write in German and even a little in Latin. As well as prayer and study the nuns also had to manage all the practical tasks in the convent – raising animals, organising menus and doing the accounts – and these were skills that Katie would find very useful in later life. What Katie had never experienced – and never expected to experience – was family life.

Katie and some of the other nuns somehow managed to get their hands on a number of Luther's writings. His teaching criticised not only the immorality of many monks and nuns but also questioned the biblical basis of the whole system. He was very critical of enforced celibacy and argued that being shut away in a convent or monastery was less pleasing to God than living for Him in the outside world. Around Germany monks and nuns were leaving their cloisters – some freely, others after daring escapes. Unfortunately for Katie her convent came under the jurisdiction of Duke George of Saxony, who had recently had a man executed for helping some fleeing nuns. It looked as though Katie was destined to live out her life in the convent. However, after a group of the discontented nuns had been refused help from their families, they decided to write directly to Luther. In April 1523 an escape plan went into action. Leonhard Koppe was a fish merchant who regularly delivered to the convent. The nine nuns were hidden among the barrels in the back of his cart and smuggled back to the safety of Wittenberg, Luther's home town. Soon four had been taken back by their families, but the rest needed to find homes as soon as possible. Wolfgang Schiefer, who lived in the town, wrote to a friend, 'Several days ago a wagon arrived here with a load of vestal virgins, as they are now called. They would like to marry as much as to stay alive. May God provide them with husbands so that in the course of time they won't run into greater need!'[2]

Some found husbands more easily than others – and Katie was particularly difficult to marry off. For an ex-nun, abandoned by her family and forced on the charity of strangers, she was extraordinarily fussy.

She was not considered beautiful, and her personality was too forceful for some. An early suitor was warned off by his family, who were horrified by the idea of a respectable man marrying a nun. Although she didn't expect to marry for love, she was not prepared to marry just anybody – particularly not the elderly Dr Glatz, who Luther had in mind for her. Luther's friend Amsdorf wrote bluntly, 'What in the devil are you up to that you try to persuade good Kate and force that old skinflint, Glatz, on her. She doesn't go for him and has neither love nor affection for him.'[3] Luther replied unsympathetically, 'If she doesn't like this one, she will just have to wait a while for another.'[4] Amsdorf knew that Katie had other plans when he wrote to another friend that Katie was 'complaining that Doctor Martinus[5] was trying every which way for her to consent to Doctor Glatz. Yet for him she had neither interest nor love. Rather (if it could so happen and be God's will) she would marry either Doctor Martinus or Domine Amsdorf.'[6] Ideally Katie wanted to marry Luther, the great man himself!

Luther didn't want to marry anybody. Just four years earlier he had been appalled by the very idea of a monk marrying, exclaiming, 'Good heaven! will our Wittenberg friends allow wives even to monks! Ah! at least they will not make *me* take a wife.'[7] Even after Katie had arrived in Wittenberg in 1524, he wrote, 'God may change my purpose, if such be his pleasure; but at present I have no thought of taking a wife.'[8] He explained why in a letter to Argula von Grumbach: 'It is not that I do not feel my flesh or sex, since I am neither wood nor stone, but my mind is far removed from marriage, since daily I expect the death and punishment due a heretic.'[9] Even though he had encouraged colleagues, such as the young Philipp Melanchthon, to marry to make a point to the Catholic authorities, Luther, at forty, seemed to be a confirmed bachelor.

So how come Katie and Martin Luther were married just a few months later in June 1525? It seemed to take Luther himself by surprise as he wrote, 'Suddenly, while I still had other thoughts, God in a wondrous way threw me into matrimony with Katharina von Bora, the nun.'[10] It certainly wasn't for romantic love. Politics definitely played a part. With the Peasants' War raging, the Reformation and Luther's life were in danger. By marrying, Luther would make the point that he had no intention of turning back to the Catholic Church, whatever happened. There were other more personal reasons. Luther wrote to his friend Amsdorf, who had encouraged the match, explaining, 'I married to gratify my father, who asked me to marry and leave him descendants ... I was not carried away by passion, for I do not love my wife that way, but esteem her as a friend.'[11] Katie had not even been his first choice of the run-away nuns. Years later he wrote, 'Had I wished to marry fourteen years ago, I should have chosen Ave von Schonfeld, now wife of Basil Axt. I never loved my wife but suspected her of being proud (as she is), but God willed me to take pity on the poor abandoned girl ...'[12] (Katie at the time was twenty-five.) Luther's friend Melanchthon, perhaps in a huff at not being invited to the small private ceremony, was less generous: 'The man is very facile and the nuns tried to inveigle him. Perhaps the much intercourse with the nuns softened and inflamed him, noble and magnanimous as he is.'[13] Henry VIII attributed even worse motives to him: 'At the instigation of the devil, the suggestions of the flesh, and the emptiness of your understanding, you have not been ashamed to violate with your sacrilegious embraces a virgin devoted to the Lord.'[14] It seems that other friends did support the marriage, but not his choice of wife! Seven years later Luther wrote, 'If I had not married secretly, all my friends would have cried, "Not this woman but somebody else!"'[15] Katie's strong personality did not go down well with some of the older generation.

At the start of her married life Katie had to cope not only with an indifferent husband and his unsupportive friends but also a vitriolic pamphlet campaign against her. One, which was widely distributed, was addressed to Katie and went like this:

> *Woe to you, poor fallen woman, not only because you have passed from light to darkness, from the*

cloistered holy religion into a damnable, shameful life, but also that you have gone from the grace to the disfavour of God, in that you have left the cloister in lay clothes and have gone to Wittenberg like a chorus girl. You are said to have lived with Luther in sin. Then you have married him, forsaking Christ your bridegroom. You have broken your vow, and by your example have reduced many godly young women in the cloisters to a pitiable state of body and of soul, despised of all men.[16]

Such hostility could have destroyed a weaker woman. Only someone as strong willed as Katie could possibly have turned the situation, and her reputation, around to become, within a few years, the much-loved role model for women of her, and future, generations.

Katie was certainly strong willed. Luther wrote, 'If I were to marry again, I would carve an obedient wife out of a block of marble, for unless I did so, I should despair of finding one.'[17] She hardly seems the model of a submissive wife. A few days after her wedding Amsdorf reported that she said, 'I have to train the doctor a little differently, so that he does what I want.'[18] Both Katie and Luther had lived in single-sex communities for many years and had little, even second-hand, experience of married life. Both were used to doing things *their* way, and were equally determined. Initially Katie's attitude alienated others in Luther's circle. A contemporary wrote, 'She was of a lofty spirit, wilful and proud; so that she did not cultivate much acquaintance and friendship with other wives, because she accounted herself above them, on account of the fame of her husband.'[19] Humanly speaking the marriage did not have great prospects. It had its unromantic origins in theology, politics and family duty, and, with two such powerful personalities involved, the relationship was never going to be conflict-free. However, within a year Luther wrote, 'She is gentle and in all things obedient and agreeable, thank God much more than I had dared hope, so that I would not exchange my poverty for the riches of Croesus.'[20] In time Katie even managed to win over most of her husband's friends and colleagues. In 1536 the Reformer Wolfgang Capito wrote, 'She has been created to keep up your health so that you may serve the church born under you, that is, all that hope in Christ ... She is deservedly esteemed because as Hausfrau she cares for our common teacher with gentleness and diligence.'[21] Over the years the marriage became far more than just a practical arrangement as Martin and Katie came to love each other deeply and delighted in the joys of family life that neither had ever expected to experience. Towards the end of his life Luther wrote, 'I love my Kate; yes I love her more than myself; that is really true; I would die rather than she and the family should die.'[22]

From such an unpromising start how was it that Katie was able to make the marriage a success and in the process become a role model for biblical womanhood? First she was determined to base her life on her growing understanding of God's Word. She wrote, 'Wedlock grounded on God's Word and a house in which God's Word comes upon the table like the daily bread, that is a blessed house.'[23] In the convent she had not been brought up to study the Bible – in fact the practice was frowned upon by the Catholic authorities. Her Latin was minimal so, until Luther himself translated the Bible into German, her access to Scripture would have been limited. Yet as soon as she could, she was determined to learn: 'I attentively listen to the reading and preaching of the Word, and I read portions of it every day; so that I am able to repeat from memory many passages from it.'[24] To encourage her, Luther bet Katie fifty guilders that she couldn't read the entire Bible by Easter one year. She wasn't satisfied just to have read it: 'I hear it enough, also read it daily, and could talk about it. Would to God I also did according to it.'[25] Katie Luther's life shows how someone can be transformed through God's grace, a determination to obey God's Word and the working of the Holy Spirit. We might feel that we are far too busy to find time to read God's Word and pray day by day – and be disappointed by the lack of growth in our Christian lives. Katie found time – even when, as we shall see, her life was overwhelmingly busy. There was no electric lighting – so reading in the evening by rush lights would have been hard. There were no electronic devices to make Bible reading more accessible – her Bible would have been vast, heavy and primitively printed. She would have faced endless interruptions and constant noise as she tried to read and pray – but she did.

The Luthers' successful marriage was certainly built on a determination to build their family life on the Bible, but also relied on Katie's capacity for hard work. After years in the monastery Martin was thoroughly undomesticated. Before he got married he would only change his sheets around once a year. Being married to Martin Luther was going to be tough – particularly as his domesticity never improved. Years later he cut up a pair of his son's new breeches so that he could patch a pair of his own – at least he was trying to help! Most of the practical side of the marriage was going to be down to Katie. Luther was very honest when he wrote, 'I'm no good at running the house, can't get used to it. Had we not this sex, the women folk, housekeeping would go to pieces. In the house I leave the rule to Kate.'[26] Thankfully Katie enjoyed a challenge. As a wedding present the couple were given the Black Cloister, Luther's monastery, as their very own place to live – as well as access to the Wittenberg wine cellars for a year! The Black Cloister was vast, with forty rooms on the first floor and with monastic cells on the floor above. As the monks had gradually left in response to Luther's teaching, the buildings and the gardens had been neglected. Many of the cloister's furnishings and fittings had been stolen, and as an ex-monk and ex-nun Katie and Martin had no possessions of their own with which to fill it. Her first task was to create a family home out of a semi-wrecked cloister meant for forty monks.

Money for the job was going to be an issue. Having taken a vow of poverty, Martin had never had to deal with money, was ridiculously generous and permanently in debt. Shortly before his marriage he wrote, 'I am becoming day by day more overwhelmed with debt. I shall be forced to beg alms by and by.'[27] The monks had been used to receiving gifts from lay people who hoped that their generosity would win them favour with God. An unfortunate result of Luther's teaching that God's favour was a gift, and could not be bought, was that charitable giving dried up. Luther still refused to accept payment for any of his preaching or writing. He wanted his printed works to be cheap to buy so that even the poor could read the good news of the gospel. (The printers had other ideas, charged high prices and kept what would have been Luther's cut for themselves.) He was reluctant to accept gifts, unless he knew they could be used to help those in greater need than himself. Had he been left to his own devices, the situation would have been disastrous. As he wrote, 'I manage my household affairs strangely, and consume more than I receive. I expend five hundred gulden in the kitchen to say nothing of clothing, ornaments and alms-giving; while my annual income is but two hundred gulden.'[28] He needed Katie's help.

Katie used her initiative from the start. She accepted at least one generous wedding gift behind Luther's back, and discouraged him from giving others away. Somehow she managed to keep track of all their incomings and outgoings. Immediately she established a kitchen garden to provide them with fruit and vegetables, and even managed to get Martin to help out. He wrote to his friend Spalatin, 'I have planted a garden and built a well very successfully.'[29] In time she persuaded Luther to buy some land with a stream running through it from which she made a fish pond that provided perch, carp, trout and pike. In 1542 we know she owned eight pigs, five cows, nine calves as well as chickens, pigeons, geese and their much-loved dog Tolpel. She also brewed her own beer, which Luther missed when he was away. In 1540 he bought a small farm for her, from her brother, at Zuhlsdorf, a few days' journey from Wittenberg, where she spent several weeks each summer. With what she produced she was able to feed the household, and sell the surplus to provide much needed extra cash.

This was particularly important as the number of people living in the Black Cloister grew. Luther was not just a preacher and leader of the international evangelical movement, he was also Professor of Theology at Wittenberg University. Like other lecturers he took in students, who for a *small* fee would get board and lodging and the benefit of his company and pearls of wisdom at meal times. Soon all the rooms were full, not only with students but also with the Luthers' own growing family (six or seven orphaned nieces and nephews, various relatives of Katie's, including Auntie Lena from the convent, and four children whose mother had died of the plague) as well as a constant stream of visiting reformers and refugees fleeing Catholic persecution. Both Martin and Katie had been used to living in large communities, but now the care of the huge household rested entirely on their, and particularly Katie's, shoulders. Her training in the convent was put to good use and she was clearly an excellent hostess as friends, students and ex-students vied for the privilege of being married from the Black Cloister, and later to have Luther as godfather to their children. Each occasion meant more expense. Katie herself had to lay on banquets for baptisms, weddings and other celebrations, sometimes for hundreds of people. Eventually she taught her husband to say 'no'. After one more request for a wedding reception, he wrote, 'My dear fellow, we just can't manage it. I would suggest that you have your banquet at Freiburg or later on here on a very modest scale.'[30]

Katie took the command to be hospitable very seriously, but some guests were easier than others. There was the regular group of theologians – or Sanhedrin as Luther called them – who came to talk over the issues of the day. There were also unexpected visitors. The aristocratic Elizabeth of Brandenburg, the King of Denmark's sister, had been locked in her room by her husband for converting to Protestantism. She escaped in the back of a peasant's cart and came to the Black Cloister for protection and sympathy, which the Luthers were happy to give. Rosina von Truchsess was another matter. She claimed to be a noble nun with nowhere to live following the closure of her convent. She was taken in and continued to stay even after it was revealed that, in fact, she was a widow whose husband had been executed as a rebel. She repaid their kindness by stealing, cheating and sleeping around. When she asked one of the Luthers' servants to help her with an abortion, enough was enough and she was sent packing – only to spend her next years slandering the family who had been so good to her!

It must have been hard for Luther and Katie to care for so many people, while also bringing up a young family of their own. It would have been easy for their children to have been neglected with all the other demands of ministry. Neither of them had expected to have children, and Katie had very little knowledge of what family life should look like – her mother died when she was tiny and she was sent away to a convent when she was only five. So it is extraordinary that the Luther's home became seen as the ideal godly household. They had no older role models to copy and no 'how to' guides to Christian parenting. They just got on with it. They showed that it was possible to follow Jesus faithfully in the mess, muddle, fun and frustration of family life, not just in the isolation of the cloister. They had six children in the space of eight years, and loved even the less appealing bits of parenthood. Martin wrote, when one of the children was in the process of being potty trained, 'Child, what have you done that I should love you so? What with your befouling the corners and bawling through the whole house?'[31] He compared Katie's love for the children with God's love for him: 'Surely God must talk with me even more fondly than my Katie with her Martinichen.'[32] They enjoyed time as a family. Luther built a bowling alley so he could play with family and friends. He was quite competitive – he commented, 'Melanchthon is a better Greek scholar than I am, but I beat him at bowling.'[33] They had musical evenings where the children sang. Luther tried to bring back presents for the family from his many trips. As parents they were a great team. Luther praised Katie at dinner, and the comment was written down by one of his admiring students and published in the famous *Table Talk*: 'The greatest happiness is to have a wife to whom you can trust your business and who is a good mother to your children. Katie you have a husband who loves you; many an empress is not so well off.'[34]

Family life was not always smooth. Perhaps their example proved more powerful as they had to cope with the pain as well as the joys of parenthood. In the sixteenth century death in infancy and childhood was common, and something that most families had to deal with. It didn't make losing a child any less heartbreaking. The Luthers' second child, Elizabeth, died when she was only a year old. Their grief was lived out in public. Katie was still having to cater for a house full of students, and one recorded, 'Because his wife was very sad [and] cried and howled, Dr Martin Luther said to her, "Dear Käthe, think about where she is going! She comes to good!"'[35] Luther too, was, grief-stricken: 'It is amazing what a sick, almost woman-like heart she has left to me. So much has grief for her overcome me ... Never before would I have believed that a father's heart could have such tender feelings for his child.'[36] Their third child, Magdalena, died when she was just thirteen. As any parents would, they battled to keep their feelings in line with their theology:

My wife and I should only give thanks with joy for such a happy departure and blessed end, by which Magdalena has escaped the power of the flesh, the world, the Turk, and the devil; yet the force of our natural love is so great that we cannot do this without weeping and grieving in our hearts or even without experiencing death ourselves ... Even the death of Christ ... is unable totally to take this away, as it should.[37]

The Luthers were honest about their struggles. They were open with others and let them see their pain. Living in a large community and having such outgoing personalities meant they probably never thought of behaving in any other way. Had they tried to hide their grief and present a perfect façade to the world, their example would have been far less powerful. God is more glorified when we acknowledge our weakness than when we pretend to be strong!

The Luthers' other daughter, Margarethe, also almost died in a measles epidemic, which killed two of the students in the house. Katie herself was seriously ill following a miscarriage when she was forty-one. After finally recovering, having spent three months in bed, she then had to care for ten students dangerously ill with a fever. If her extended family wasn't enough to deal with, she also visited those who were sick in the rest of Wittenberg. Thankfully the three boys, Hans, Martin and Paul, were all quite healthy! Martin was not.

Throughout Martin's married life he suffered from

kidney stones, acute earache and depression, as well as other sporadic illnesses. In a time before painkillers and antibiotics even minor ailments could be unbearable. Anyone who has suffered earache will sympathise with Luther's condition: 'The pain attacked my life. The unbearable pains pressed tears out of me – Something I don't easily do; and I said to the Lord, "Either put an end to the pain or put an end to me."'[38] Katie fed him, cared for him and sometimes bullied him into health – and at times prepared for his possible death. His depression was probably the hardest thing for her to deal with. At the best of times he could be difficult, as he admitted: 'I know full well Dr Martin Luther is a poor sinful man and has brought into the wedded life also his sin, especially his violent, explosive temper.'[39] His low moods were harder to bear. Even when he was well, he would lock himself in his study for days with nothing to eat; when he was not well, the Cloister's whole atmosphere would change. Katie developed her own strategies for coping. On one occasion she hired a locksmith to remove his study door. On another she dressed in black mourning clothes. When Luther asked her who had died, she replied that God had! She stated, 'He must have died, or my Martin would not be so sorrowful.'[40] Those tactics might not have worked with everyone, but they did with Luther.

Undoubtedly Martin lived longer and was able to work more effectively because of Katie's care, common sense and practical hard work. The letters he wrote to her show how much he valued all she did. He addressed letters not only to his 'Dear Katharina' and his 'Dear wife' but also 'To the rich lady of Zulsdorf, Frau Doctor Katherine Luther ...' or 'To my heartily beloved wife Katherine Luther, Zulsdorfian Doctoress, swine-marketian, and whatever else she may be ...'[41] He wrote to her about his health and her beer, but also about the theological issues he was discussing with the Zwinglians when he was in Marburg. He expected her to understand, and valued her opinions.[42] Eventually Luther's poor health caught up with him when he was away travelling once again. Katie was worried about him – Martin addressed one of his final letters 'To the saintly, anxious-minded lady Katherine Luther'. He teased her that by worrying she had caused a series of bad things to happen. Certainly by worrying she couldn't stop the thing she dreaded. On 18 February 1546, soon after writing her a last letter, he died.

Katie was devastated. She wrote to her sister, 'I am truly so cast down that I cannot tell the troubles of my heart to anyone and do not know what to make of it all. I cannot eat or drink or sleep.'[43] Martin had always worried about what would happen to her after he died. Despite the international spread of his ideas, the people of Wittenberg had become half-hearted and resented the reformers' stress on personal faith and high standards of morality. Once Luther had gone he was worried, quite rightly, that Katie would not be welcome. He had left debts, which creditors hounded her to pay. In his will he had, very unusually, left everything to Katie, rather than the children. The chancellor of Wittenberg disputed the will and tried to deny Katie custody of the children. To top it all the Schmalkaldic War broke out between Lutheran and Catholic states, forcing the family to flee. They returned during a lull in the fighting to find that their home and all their property had been ruined. Soon they had to escape the war zone again, and when she finally returned, Katie was shunned. Nobody wanted to help the wife of the great reformer with Catholic troops in the neighbourhood. Ever practical, she restored a small house they owned in the town, and once again took in lodgers. An ex-boarder at the Black Cloister wrote, 'I often think on that man of God, Dr Martin Luther, how he made his wife commit to memory Psalm xxxi, when she was young, vigorous, and cheerful, and could not then know how this psalm would afterwards be so sweet and consolatory to her. But her beloved spouse did this with good reason, for he well knew that after his death she would be an afflicted and miserable woman, and would greatly need the comfort contained in that psalm.'[44] The words of this psalm are in many ways similar to those of Luther's famous hymn 'A mighty fortress is our God', which is based on Psalm 46. Both speak of God's protection in the midst of opposition and danger.

A mighty fortress is our God, a bulwark never
failing;
Our helper He, amid the flood of mortal ills
prevailing:
For still our ancient foe doth seek to work us woe;
His craft and power are great, and, armed with
cruel hate,
On earth is not his equal ...
That word above all earthly powers, no thanks to
them, abideth;
The Spirit and the gifts are ours through Him
Who with us sideth:
Let goods and kindred go, this mortal life also;
The body they may kill: God's truth abideth still,
His kingdom is forever.[45]

Katie needed that eternal perspective as the last years of her life continued to be stressful and insecure. Just a few years later she had to flee her home once again, this time because of the plague. Travelling in a cart with all her worldly goods, the horse bolted, throwing Katie into a ditch. Although she was faithfully nursed by her eighteen-year-old daughter Margarethe, she never recovered. She died in December 1552. The preacher at her funeral took the opportunity to attack the townspeople for the shameful way she had been treated. Luther's friend Melanchthon praised her faith: 'During all her illness she had found comfort in God's Word, calmly looking for another life, commending her children to the Lord, and praying the Holy Spirit to re-establish that unity of doctrine which had been the object of the efforts of her pious husband.'[46]

Katie would have most appreciated Martin's earlier tribute to his wife: 'When I look at all the women in the world, I find none that I can praise as I can praise mine with a cheerful conscience.'[47] A woman who started life as a nun, the ideal woman of medieval Catholicism, had almost single-handedly created a new ideal for the Protestant age – a godly woman, working alongside her husband, supporting him in ministry and bringing up their children to trust in Jesus. That she also managed to run a farm, a brewery, a hotel and a hospital, as well as deal with a charismatic, depressive husband in the forefront of international events, makes her a fairly terrifying role model – for a role few now would want to fill. Looking at her amazing life it is easy to miss how her example can inspire every one of us – whatever our gifts, status or gender – by how an ordinary, self-centred and wilful sinner was willing to obey God's Word and be transformed by God's Spirit into the person He wanted her to be.

BIBLE STUDY
& REFLECTION
Ephesians 4:17 – 5:2

1. In what way was Katie's early life in the convent similar to that described in verses 17–18?

2. How did Katie 'come to know Christ' (v. 20)?

3. How was your experience similar or different to hers?

4. Having come to Christ, how was she then able to be 'taught in him in accordance with the truth that is in Jesus' (v. 21)?

5. How does your attitude to God's Word compare to Katie's?

6. What bits of her 'old self' (v. 22) did Katie particularly need to put off?

7. In what way do you need 'to put off your old self'?

8. Looking at the list in verses 25–32, how far had Katie been 'made new' (v. 23) during her life?

9. Which areas are still a work in progress for you? How can you ensure that you are a life-long learner like Katie and don't get stuck in a rut?

CHAPTER TWO

Anna Zwingli
1484–1538
A Downtrodden Disciple

We know loads about Katie Luther. Her husband was the star of the Protestant Reformation and they became the celebrity couple of their generation. Their relationship was lived out in public and we can get to know Katie through Martin's many letters, as well as through the memories of those who shared their home. She was also an exceptional woman in her own right, who carved out a new role for herself, and for millions of other women who came after her. We know far less about Anna Zwingli, the wife of Ulrich Zwingli, leader of the Swiss Reformation. Her husband, at the time, was almost as famous as Katie's, but their marriage was a much more private affair. Zwingli was less affectionate and wrote fewer letters, and Anna was less of a trail-blazer.

Like most women in the sixteenth century Anna's life was lived in response to the decisions and actions of men. Today we might pity someone with so little independence, and so few choices. Her life was at times almost unbearably hard. In fact one writer has said that she was 'doomed to be … the most cruelly tried of all the women whose memory has been preserved to us by history'.[1] Yet God not only used her in unexpected ways but also sustained her through all the difficult circumstances over which she had no control.

Ulrich Zwingli[2] was the same age as Martin Luther but, other than that, the two men had very little in common. Luther was from eastern Germany, a region of princes and dukes. Zwingli was from the mountains of Switzerland, a confederation of states ruled by powerful guilds and councils. Although Luther had been a monk and Zwingli a Roman Catholic priest, their attitudes and outlook towards the faith in their youth had been very different. Both were very well educated, but Luther's background was mainly in medieval scholasticism while Zwingli had been taught in the modern humanist way. The scholastics' authority were the theologians and philosophers of the middle ages while the humanists were excited by the classical world, and saw Greek and Roman literature and philosophy as the source books of modern civilisation. While Luther had studied the Bible in a desperate attempt to understand how he, a sinful wretch, could be acceptable to a holy God, Zwingli studied the Bible as the source book of Christianity.

Although both became leaders of the Reformation, their emphases were quite different. Luther's key theme in all he did was justification by faith alone — the doctrine that had helped him trust that God could accept even him. In contrast Zwingli stressed the importance of Scripture alone — a passion to see everything done in line with the Word of God. Luther experienced a dramatic conversion, while Zwingli's rejection of Catholic teaching came much more gradually. While Luther, before his conversion, had been wracked with guilt over the tiniest things, Zwingli for a long time was unaware of even his most glaring sins.

In Zwingli's growing understanding of the Bible's teaching he took a remarkably long time to grasp some things that, to us, might seem blindingly obvious. As a priest Zwingli was not allowed to marry — but he did not see why that should stop him being a ladies' man. He was not unusual. A few years later an evangelical writer commented that while married priests were thrown out of the church, the bishops 'allow the rest, whether burdened by adultery, fornication, sodomy or with whores ... to celebrate Mass every day'.[3] There were rumours of Zwingli having several affairs in his first parish. When he was offered the job at the main church in Zurich, he had to defend himself against the allegation that he had seduced a respectable girl. His defence was that the girl was not respectable! He wrote, 'It was a case of maiden by day, matron by night, and not so much of the maiden by day but everybody in Einsiedeln knew about her ... no one in Einsiedeln thought I had corrupted a maiden.'[4] He still got the job as his competitor for the post was openly living with his mistress and had six children. He did try to restrain himself and found that studying classical literature helped: 'This hard work takes the heat out of such sensual desires even if it does not entirely eliminate them.'[5]

Little by little Zwingli saw that his lifestyle needed to match up to his increasingly biblical preaching. He also came to see that the Bible allowed ministers to marry. Marriage could be the answer to Zwingli's problem. In 1522 Zwingli and a group of other ministers put two and two together when they wrote to the bishop asking for him to permit ministers to marry and argued, 'How will the simple-minded common man believe in him who even while he preaches the Gospel to them is thought by them to be licentious and a shameless dog?'[6]

This was a real issue for Zwingli. By this time he was the most influential reformer in Zurich, and even in Switzerland. He preached constantly – biblical expositions for the townspeople, and market-day sermons for the less educated who came in from the countryside. Thousands flocked to hear him. In January 1522 he had also started living with a widow called Anna Reinhard. That few were shocked shows how common it was for priests to have mistresses, but Zwingli knew that the Bible taught that he had to be either married or celibate – he was neither.

Anna was, at that time, what was known as a priest's whore – a de facto wife without rights or respectability. She was a widow in her late thirties, and although relatively well off, she was still in a vulnerable place in society – needing a male protector for herself and her children, but in no position to be choosy as to whom that protector would be.

Anna's first marriage had also been controversial. In 1504 she married Hans Meyer von Knonau, a young man from a wealthy and respected Zurich family. Someone from that background would have been expected to have a marriage arranged by his parents, but Hans fell in love with Anna. Unfortunately Anna's family was not wealthy and respected enough – her father was an inn keeper – and Hans was disinherited. For years he had no contact with his family, no allowance and no prospect of inheriting any of his father's wealth. He now had to make his own way in the world, which he managed quite successfully. In 1510 he became a member of the Great Council of 200 in Zurich and an important citizen in his own right. Anna and Hans had three children in three years, and, perhaps in order to pay for the growing family, in 1513 Hans signed up as a mercenary, fighting for the Pope's army against the French. (Being a mercenary was an acceptable job for the Swiss; Zwingli himself had earlier served as a mercenary chaplain, for which he won a commendation from the Pope.) When Hans returned to Zurich, his health was poor, perhaps the result of wounds received in battle, perhaps just illness. He died in 1517, leaving Anna a widow with three young children – Gerold was eight, Margaretha was seven and Agatha just five.

Anna's situation was less bleak than it might have been due to a chance encounter with her father-in-law a few years earlier. When Gerold was a toddler, a servant took him to the fish market in Zurich. His grandfather was sitting outside an inn, watching the world go by, when he saw the little boy playing. Apparently Gerold was such a striking child that the old man asked who he was. When he found out that he was his own grandson, he went home with him, met Anna and from then on was reconciled to the family. He decided to raise Gerold himself and help with his education. The boy went to live with his grandparents, and even after his grandfather's death, he continued to live with his grandmother. We don't know what Anna made of this arrangement – it must have been very hard to hand over her little boy – but after Hans' death, it gave the family more security, and eventually it seems Anna may have inherited the family home.

By 1518 Anna was living near Zwingli's home in the church courtyard in Zurich, and Gerold was going to the school attached to the church. As a humanist Zwingli was always passionate about education, and was keen to encourage talented youngsters. Gerold was particularly gifted and in 1520 Zwingli helped him to go to Basel, the main educational centre in Switzerland, when he was just eleven. His teacher in Basel was very impressed and wrote to Zwingli, 'Have you many Zurichers like this Meyer? Send them all to me ... May God preserve this one and all his like to you, and to me, and to the country.'[7] Zwingli probably got to know Anna through his interest in Gerold, and also as a member of his large congregation. Given his eye for pretty women, and the fact that Anna was apparently very beautiful, he might well have shown her more interest than the mothers of other students. By 1522 they were living together.

This may have been accepted by many of his parishioners, used to the low moral standards of the Catholic clergy, but some thought he set a very poor example. Martin Bucer, the influential reformer, wrote to Zwingli after his eventual marriage, 'You were thought to be a fornicator by some, and by others held to have little faith in Christ.'[8] Other members of the clergy were getting married, despite the possibility of excommunication and even imprisonment. Zwingli was certainly prepared to stand up to the church authorities over other issues. In Lent 1522 Zwingli was involved in the infamous 'Affair of the Sausages', when a group of protesters publicly ate meat during the Lenten fast. So why did Zwingli not just marry Anna as it seems he wanted? We don't really know, but it certainly left her in a difficult position. While it was her lowly background that caused problems with her first marriage, it may be that her higher social status through the Meyer family made it impossible for her to marry a priest. There were certainly legal issues over her inheritance after the wedding. Almost all of the first pastors' wives came from socially vulnerable groups – ex-nuns, priests' concubines or housekeepers, and poor widows. Had she been a little bit *more* vulnerable, she might have been married sooner.

Anna had no choice in the matter. She had had no choice either when her father-in-law effectively adopted her son or when Zwingli decided it was best for him to be sent away to school. Anna, like most sixteenth-century women, had very few choices. Her life was decided and defined by men. Despite her powerlessness, she had a very important role to play in Reformation history. From the moment they got together God used Anna to keep Zwingli on the straight and narrow. Even before they were legally married this relationship kept him away from temptation, gave his ministry consistency and so paved the way for Zurich to become the centre for the Reformation in Switzerland. He later wrote, from personal experience,

> *It is a dangerous thing for a young priest to have access, through the sanctity of his office, to young women, be they married or virgins. Let straw be kept from fire. Give the priest a wife; he would then, like any other honest man, concern himself with the care of his household, his wife, his child, and other affairs, whereby he would be freed from many trials and temptations.*[9]

After 1522 there were no more allegations of immorality laid at Zwingli's door.

Eventually on 4 April 1524 the couple were married, with Anna six months pregnant with their first child! Bucer, who had been one of the first reformers to marry, and was always encouraging his friends to do the same, was delighted: 'When I learned from your letter to Capito that you had publicly celebrated your marriage, I was out of myself with joy.'[10] Capito, a fellow reformer, prayed at the wedding that Anna would be 'a fellow-servant in the Word, a help-meet of an apostle'.[11] Zwingli's evangelical colleagues finally thought he had done the right thing.

Others disagreed. Zwingli was criticised for marrying for money. This was a common and sometimes justified criticism of the marrying priests. As alms from pious Catholics dried up, they needed an alternative source of income — often rich widows fitted the bill. Zwingli quickly wrote in his own, and Anna's, defence,

I am compelled, by the injustice of my enemies, to speak of my wife Anna Reinhard, whom these stupid men declare to be exceedingly rich. The truth is, that with the exception of clothes and female ornaments, she has not more than four hundred gold coins. And though she possesses splendid dresses, rings and other jewels, yet, from the day that she became my wife, she has never worn any of these, but has chosen to conform herself to the dress of other respectable matrons of our city. Those things which she receives for her support from her children (for the family of her ancestors is illustrious) she cannot well reject; especially as she has now attained her fortieth year.[12]

Zwingli clearly needed a wife if he was to settle down and become a respectable church leader, no longer dogged by scandal – but did it matter who that wife was? Was Anna's only function to keep him from disgracing himself? Anna may not have had any control over the big decisions in her life, but in this letter we can see that there were areas where Anna could make choices of her own, and that those choices made a difference. It would have been natural for her to have wanted to cling onto the last vestiges of her previous and more privileged life, but Zwingli says she 'has chosen' to wear the simple clothes of the other women in the town. This choice would have immediately endeared her to her husband's congregation, as well as putting an end to the jibes at Zwingli's motives for marrying. However powerless we may feel we are, we are all able to make a difference by making godly choices in the small decisions we face each day.

Zwingli said that his ideal woman was 'so pleasant in nature as to soften a rough man'.[13] In Anna he found such a woman. The wayward womaniser became a devoted family man. Zwingli was a loving father and wrote down the dates of their four children's birthdays and baptisms in the front of his Greek Bible. Despite his disapproval of instrumental music in church, at home he put it to good use: 'Music, which I have diligently cultivated from boyhood, often renders me good service with the children, in putting them in good humour or sending them to sleep.'[14] Zwingli still liked a good party. They held musical gatherings in their home and took part in city banquets and processions. When Zwingli was criticised for having fun, he reminded his hearers of Jesus at the wedding at Cana. Nonetheless life with Anna tamed him.

Together they settled into a domestic routine. Zwingli had the normal preaching and pastoral responsibilities as the pastor of a large church, but he managed his time so that he could spend time with family and friends. On a quiet day, with no significant business, he would read the Bible and pray early in the morning, then go to church to preach. They ate their main meal at 11 a.m. and then spent time as a family, received visitors or went for a walk, before Zwingli studied (always standing up) during the afternoon. After supper there was more time for family and friends. Zwingli often worked through the night to get everything else done – which perhaps explains the rather haphazard style of some of his writing.

Quiet days were rare. The house was usually full, not only of friends but also of visiting theologians and exiles from around Europe. One historian has described it well: 'What a piebald host of men from the various countries of Europe received liberal supplies for body and soul in the simple house of the parish priest at the Great Minster.'[15] Early on in her life with Zwingli

Anna had to cope with controversial guests. Ulrich von Hutten had accepted Luther's teaching and had tried to impose the Reformation by force in what has become known as the Knights' Revolt. When it failed, he asked his former mentor, the famous humanist Erasmus, for help. He refused. Dying from syphilis, friendless and poverty stricken, Hutten eventually came to Zurich. The Zwinglis cared for him, paid for him to go to healing springs for treatment and, when this failed, organised for him to stay with friends on a remote island in Lake Zurich, where he died soon after. Hutten's arch-enemy, Ulrich, Duke of Wurttemberg, also came to stay. The duke had murdered Hutten's cousin, so that he could marry his wife. For this, as well as general bad government, he had been kicked out of Wurttemberg. He, too, found sanctuary with the Zwinglis. During his time with them, through their hospitality and Zwingli's preaching, he was converted. He later became one of the key political leaders of the Reformation in Germany. The impact of hospitality in a Christian home can't be underestimated! Years later another visitor, Nicholas Arator, wrote, 'In Zwingli's household among these dear friends, I was so well pleased with their Christian family life that I can never forget it as long as I live, and that I shall always commend it to my own.'[16] In her own quiet way Anna Zwingli was making a difference.

It is not surprising that Arator was impressed with Anna's family. She had three children from her first marriage, who were ten, twelve and fourteen years old when she moved in with Zwingli. Gerold in particular was a star. He seems to have been both godly, gifted and very grown up! He got married at the unusually young age of sixteen to a girl the same age. His wife was described in the family papers as a 'God-fearing, handsome, intelligent and admirable woman'.[17] When he was only eighteen, he became a member of the Council of 200 – like his father – and when he was just twenty-one, he became its president. Anna had four more children with Zwingli – all born when she was in her forties. Their priority was to bring up the children as Christians. One daughter was born while Zwingli was away at the Berne disputation and he wrote to Anna, 'Grace and peace from God, dearest wife. I praise God that He hath given you a happy delivery. He will grant us grace to bring up our little daughter according to His will.'[18] She did a good job as a mother. Three of the children survived to adulthood. They were all involved in ministry. Regula became a much-loved pastor's wife; William died of the plague while studying for ordained ministry; and Huldreich became a deacon of his father's church and professor of theology.

Anna took her role as Zwingli's wife seriously. As the proofs of the Swiss-German version of Luther's Bible arrived, Zwingli read them to her, and gave her a copy as soon as it was complete. She then aimed to introduce the new Bible to as many of the families in the congregation as she could. Literacy in a town like Zurich was far higher than in the countryside, but people, particularly women of her generation, had been discouraged from reading the Bible for themselves. She shared Zwingli's passion that faith should be based on God's Word alone – for that to happen as many as possible needed to get hold of the new translation of the Bible.

She supported her husband's work, but he never fully took her into his confidence. Unlike Martin and Katie Luther, theirs was never a real partnership of equals. As the leader of the Swiss Reformation, Zwingli was involved in all the political and theological disputes of the day. This often involved dangerous journeys and weeks away from home. In 1529 Zwingli secretly travelled to a meeting in Marburg to try to come to some agreement on the nature of the Lord's Supper, about which he and Luther violently disagreed. The Zurich City Council thought it was too risky and had tried to stop him from going. He went anyway, even though it meant travelling through Catholic territory where there were many who wanted him dead. Unlike Luther, who shared everything with Katie, Zwingli doesn't seem to have discussed the issues or even his plans with Anna. He didn't even tell her that he was going. Once he was well on his way, he asked a friend to tell her what was going on: 'Have Master Stou say to my wife whatever ought to be said to a woman, for when I left I told her only that I was going to Basel on business.'[19]

Had Zwingli told her, Anna may well have tried to stop him from making the journey. She was well aware of the constant danger he was in, even when he was at home. There were many Catholics in Zurich itself who would go to any lengths to get rid of the great reformer. They received an anonymous letter warning them of a plot to poison him: 'The perfidious wretches, not daring to attack thee openly, have fallen upon this means to remove thee from the earth, and will put poison, secretly if they can, into thy food … If thou art hungry, eat only of bread which thy own cook has baked; out of thy house, thou canst not with safety eat anything.'[20] Their friend Myconius described how drunks 'once attacked … during the night with stones, dashed in the windows, and made, what with oaths and stones together, such an infernal noise, that not one of the neighbours ventured to open a window. Nor did they desist until they ran out of stones, voice and strength.'[21] In the middle of one night there was a knock at the door and Zwingli was asked to come urgently to visit a dying parishioner. He was so tired they couldn't wake him. The next morning they discovered that this had been a plot to kidnap him. Men had been waiting to gag and bind him, before bundling him onto a ship! After this Anna always made sure she found someone to accompany her husband when he went out at night to visit the sick or dying. Zwingli appreciated her care and called her his 'Angel wife'.

It always seemed possible that Zwingli would come to a violent end. Early on the threat may have come from a jealous husband or protective father; later there was the possibility of assassination by theological or political opponents. In the end Zwingli, the evangelical pastor, died on the battlefield. In 1531 the divisions between the Catholic and Reformed cantons of Switzerland grew deeper until eventually they led to war. The people of Zurich were ill prepared. An amateur and badly equipped force of a thousand men went out to face eight thousand trained soldiers. Zwingli went as their chaplain, even though he knew it was hopeless: 'The cause is good, but ill defended; my life, as well as the lives of many excellent men who have wished to restore religion to its primitive simplicity, will be sacrificed.'[22] He was right. It was a bloodbath, and once the Catholic forces realised who Zwingli was, he was brutally killed, his body mutilated and burnt with dung. Zwingli died with twenty-five other ministers from Zurich. To make matters worse anti-Protestant riots broke out in the town as people tried to win the favour of the victorious Catholic forces. For Anna the bad news kept coming. She lost not only her husband but also her son Gerold — at twenty-two already the father of three children — her son-in-law, her brother and her brother-in-law. On hearing the news of first Zwingli's and then Gerold's death, she cried out, 'O God! Strengthen me for this trying hour. Thus is my house made desolate. Thus are the tenderest ties that bind me to the world dissevered.'[23]

How could she possibly cope with such a tragedy? Unlike Katie Luther, Anna does not come across as a particularly strong woman. Aged forty-seven she was now widowed for a second time, with three young children and two sets of fatherless grandchildren to care for. All the male members of her family, who could have taken her in and protected her, were now dead. Capito understood her predicament: 'My dearest lady, I feel for your grief and suffering, as you can imagine ... You have lost your husband, that precious man, as well as your son, son-in-law, brother-in-law, and brother. Who would not commiserate with you?'[24] In her grief three things sustained her — her faith, her friends and her family.

Soon after her bereavement Anna wrote, 'God is faithful, who will not suffer his people to be tried above what they are able; but will with the trial also make a way to escape, that they may be able to bear it.'[25] This clear reference to 1 Corinthians 10:13 shows that she knew her Bible well, and to be able to claim this promise in such an extreme situation shows that she had a deep personal trust in God. In his letter of condolence Simpert Schenk encouraged her to trust in Christ:

> *What calamitous and mournful days! ... O pious, beloved woman, be faithful; neither you nor we have lost Zwingle [Zwingli] and the others; for he who believeth in Christ hath everlasting*

life ... When you find your beloved Zwingle no longer present in the house with the children and yourself, nor in the pulpit, nor in the meetings of the learned, I beseech you, be not discouraged, nor too much grieved. Remember that he is in the house of God above, with all the children of God, and that there he listens to the mouth of Wisdom itself, and to the discourse of angels.[26]

———————————◆·◆·◆———————————

That is the letter of a true friend, and Anna was blessed with many others. Heinrich Bullinger, one of Zwingli's pupils, took over his church in Zurich. Bullinger was only twenty-seven, with a young family of his own, but he did not hesitate to welcome Anna and the children into his home. He wrote, 'You shall not want, dear mother. I will remain your friend, your teacher and adviser.'[27] He was true to his word. In all there were fifteen in the new Bullinger household, but despite the expense and the hassle, the Zwingli children were brought up as his own, even after Anna's death. Anna had been a hospitable friend to many, and now it was their turn to care for her.

Anna's life had always revolved around her home and family. With no public role to fulfil, declining health and little money, she now rarely left the house except to go to church. She focused on looking after her children and grandchildren, and comforting her widowed daughter and daughter-in-law. She died seven years after her husband at the age of fifty-four. Bullinger wrote, 'I desire no more happy end of life. She passed away softly, like a mild light, and went home to her Lord, worshipping, and commending us all to God.'[28]

In many ways Anna's life was unexceptional. She was married to an exceptional man and was the mother to several exceptional children, but Anna's own achievements were minimal. As a sixteenth-century woman she experienced life as a second-class citizen. She was not expected to understand her husband's work, she had no say in most of the decisions that profoundly affected her life and she was the victim of events beyond her control – nevertheless she was used by God in significant and surprising ways. By marrying Zwingli she removed him from past temptations and made it possible for him to become one of the most influential Christian leaders of his day. She learned to trust in Christ in all circumstances and so was able to survive the multiple tragedies she faced with her faith intact. Women today have many more rights and far higher expectations, but life will not always deliver what we expect – there will inevitably be disappointments and sadnesses. Anna Zwingli can show us that God is a faithful Father even when life is at its bleakest and that He can use even the most downtrodden disciples to fulfil his purposes.

BIBLE STUDY & REFLECTION

James 1:2–12

1. What particular trials (v. 2) did Anna face during her lifetime?

2. How do these compare to those you have faced?

3. How does Anna's life show that this 'testing of [her] faith' (v. 3) really did develop perseverance and maturity (vv. 3–4)?

4. How can looking over her whole life encourage us as we face our own trials day by day?

5. In what ways was Anna 'in humble circumstances' (v. 9)?

6. What was the 'high position' (v. 9) she could take pride in?

7. How can this encourage those of us who, perhaps like Anna, feel our lives lack significance?

8. How would Anna's life have made her particularly aware of the truth of verse 11?

9. How did the truths outlined in verse 12 encourage her in later life?

10. How can a focus on the fragility of this life and the certainty of the next help us as we face 'trials of many kinds' (v. 1)?

CHAPTER THREE

Argula von Grumbach
1492–1554
A Battling Believer

Although in some way the lives of Anna Zwingli and Katie Luther were very hard, in other ways we might be tempted to envy them. Many Christian women today can only dream of being married to such godly men. It's easy to think that if we were married to a great Christian leader, we, too, would experience vibrant faith, enthusiastic service and an amazing prayer life — but we're not, so we persuade ourselves we can be content with half-hearted discipleship.

Argula von Grumbach, like many Christian women today, was married to a man who was not only not a minister but was not a Christian either. He was not just apathetic towards her faith, he was positively antagonistic — but she did not let that stop her. In the sixteenth century women were not expected to think independently. They were certainly not expected to express their opinions in public. If they did, there could be serious consequences. Nonetheless Argula von Grumbach stood firm for the gospel, whatever the cost, throughout her life.

Argula von Stauff was born in 1492 into an aristocratic, but not particularly wealthy, family in Bavaria in Germany. German nobles at that time were notoriously uncultured — they were renowned for their fighting, swearing, drinking and womanising. Argula's family seems to have been a rare exception. Hers was a home where politics, religion and literature were discussed, and where education was valued for both boys and girls. Her brothers went to university, which was impossible even for an aristocratic girl, but at least Argula *was* taught to read and write in German at a young age. Well before Luther hit the scene, when she was just ten, Argula's father gave her a copy of a German Bible. He was clearly a forward-thinking man, who encouraged his daughter to be up with the latest controversial ideas. Argula was more conservative. She refused to read the Bible as she had been warned by Catholic clergy that it would be a bad influence on her! She later wrote, 'My dear lord and father insisted on me reading it, giving me it when I was ten years old. Unfortunately I did not obey him, being seduced by the afore-named clerics ... who said that I would be led astray.'[1]

We don't know when exactly Argula did begin to read the Bible for herself or come into contact with Protestant ideas. It may have been at the court in Munich, where she was sent at the age of fifteen to be lady-in-waiting to the sister of Emperor Frederick III. (Aristocratic boys and girls were often sent to one of the many courts in Germany as a sort of finishing school to learn good manners and make important contacts for later life.) Queen Kunigunde, Argula's boss, was always willing to consider new ideas, and may have encouraged her protégé to do the same.

She may well have been more prepared to read the Bible her beloved father gave her when, not long after she had arrived at court, both her parents died of the plague within five days of each other. She stayed at court, with her uncle Hieronymus as her guardian. Her friend from court, the future Duke Wilhelm of Bavaria, also promised to look out for her. She later reminded him, 'In my distress I was consoled by your Princely

Grace with these words, "I should not cry so much, for your Princely Grace would be my father as well as my Prince."[2] She certainly needed his support when a few years later Uncle Hieronymus was involved in a court plot. He was arrested, brutally tortured and executed. This was in 1516, still a year before Luther famously posted his ninety-five theses on the church door at Wittenberg, and symbolically began what we know as the Protestant Reformation. With so much tragedy and uncertainty in her life, it is not surprising that an educated young woman like Argula would be attracted to the radical new ideas emerging from Wittenberg.

At the time it seemed unlikely that she would have the opportunity to develop her interest. In the same year Argula was married off to Friedrich von Grumbach. He was not badly off financially, and was relatively well connected. He had various properties in Bavaria and was the administrator of the town of Dietfurt – a job that required almost no work, but which paid quite well. It was probably an arranged marriage, but anyway Argula would have had few choices. At twenty-four she was quite old to get married and she was an orphan whose guardian had been executed for treason – she was probably lucky anyone would marry her at all. At the time Friedrich might have felt the same. Yet he was sickly and poorly educated, and perhaps thought that a cultured woman from the court was quite a catch.

Over the next few years they had four children – George, Hans-Georg, Gottfried and Apollonia. From the start Argula seems to have been responsible for the family finances and fully involved in helping her husband with the administration of the estates, as well as caring for her children and organising their education. The likelihood was that her life would carry on in the same way – coping with a mismatched marriage, dealing with tenants, hiring and firing servants, caring for young children and writing to and supporting them as they grew older.

Two things stopped that from happening. First was her growing commitment to the new evangelical movement. At the time barrel-loads of Protestant pamphlets were being smuggled into Bavaria, and there were small groups springing up to discuss the new ideas in every town. Her husband, who may well have been illiterate, was vehemently opposed to her new faith. They could have continued with an uneasy truce on religious matters if it wasn't for the second key event.

In March 1522 a law was passed in Bavaria outlawing Lutheran ideas. This law was largely ignored, particularly in university towns where students had become used to debating the views they read about in the illegal pamphlets. The authorities cracked down. After various warnings eighteen-year-old Arsacius Seehofer was arrested in the university town of Ingolstadt and sentenced to be burned at the stake if he would not renounce Protestantism. In a climate of fear further arrests followed. Eventually Seehofer publically, and tearfully, renounced his faith on 7 September 1523. He escaped burning, but was imprisoned in a distant monastery. When Argula heard the news, she was furious – not only about the persecution but also about the lack of support Seehofer received from other Protestants elsewhere in Germany. Most people, then and now, would feel momentarily appalled and then just get on with everyday life – not Argula. Faced with injustice, she was determined to act. She immediately travelled sixty miles, with her four young children in tow, to visit the famous reformer Osiander in Nuremberg in order to encourage him to speak out on Seehofer's behalf. He was sympathetic, but did nothing. Argula would not let it rest. As soon as she got home on 20 September, she wrote one letter to the university authorities and another to her friend Duke Wilhelm, the ruler of all Bavaria. In a similar situation we might dash off an angry email or sign a petition online – Argula's letter to the university takes up sixteen printed pages in a modern edition, and the letter to Duke Wilhelm over twelve. Both letters are well thought out and supported by dozens of scriptural references. The impact was instant. Initially handwritten copies of the letter were circulated, but soon they were being printed in vast quantities. Fourteen editions of her letter to the

University of Ingolstadt were published in the space of just two months, twenty-nine within a year. She became a celebrity overnight.

She argued that Seehofer could not be convicted of heresy for following Luther, when all Luther was doing was pointing people towards the Bible: 'Are you not ashamed that [Seehofer] had to deny all the writings of Martin, who put the New Testament into German, simply following the text? That means that the holy Gospel and the Epistles and the story of the Apostles and so on are all dismissed by you as heresy.'[3] She continued:

> *I beseech you for the sake of God, and exhort you by God's judgement and righteousness, to tell me in writing which of the articles written by Martin or Melanchthon you consider heretical. In German not a single one seems heretical to me. And the fact is that a great deal has been published in German, and I've read it all.*[4]

The university authorities never replied to the letter. Criticism from a woman was beneath contempt, and didn't even need to be considered, however justified it might be. Sermons were preached against her. One Ingolstadt preacher referred to her as 'an insolent daughter of Eve, a heretical bitch and a confounded rogue'.[5] Others used similar insults: 'you female desperado', 'you arrogant devil', 'you shameless whore'. She had death threats. In a later letter to the Ingolstadt Council she wrote, 'I hear that some are so angry with me that they do not know how best to speed my passage from life into death.'[6] Her appeal to Duke Wilhelm fell on deaf ears. In a letter to a friend Luther wrote, 'The Duke of Bavaria rages above measure, killing, crushing and persecuting the gospel with all his might. That most noble woman, Argula von Stauffer, is there making a most valiant fight with great spirit, boldness of speech and knowledge of Christ.'[7] Her family was not supportive either. In a letter to her mother's cousin she wrote that her letter to the university ... 'made you more than a little angry with me. Perhaps you thought it unbecoming of me as a foolish woman. Which is, of course, exactly how I see myself.'[8] In the same letter it is clear that her husband was less than pleased with her actions too: 'I have heard that you are reported as saying that if my own husband would not do it, some relative should act, and wall me up. But don't believe him. Alas, he is doing far too much to persecute Christ in me.'[9] In order to punish her, her husband was stripped of his role as administrator of Dietfurt, which Luther imagined must have made her situation far worse: 'Her husband, who treats her tyrannically, has been deposed from his prefecture. What he will do you can imagine.'[10]

She must have known that such a public stand in favour of the gospel, in an area where evangelical views were illegal, would have such consequences. Why did she do it? As a woman, and as a mother, she appears partly to have been motivated by compassion for Arsacius. She wrote, 'You have forgotten one thing: that he is only eighteen years old, and still a child.'[11] She was also frustrated by the silence of others. She knew how controversial it would be for a woman to enter the public sphere, but when no one else did anything, she felt compelled to write: 'But now that I cannot see any man who is up to it, who is either willing or able to speak ... I claim for myself Isaiah 3: "I will send children to be their princes; and women, or those who are womanish, shall rule over them."'[12] From Scripture she argued that it was the duty of both men and women to stand up for the gospel: '"Whoever is ashamed of me and my words, I too will be ashamed of when I come in my majesty" [Luke 9:26] etc. Words like these, coming from the very mouth of God, are always before my eyes. For they exclude neither woman nor man.'[13] In the end she wrote the letters because she could, and believed that she should. She was not the best educated or the most articulate; she was a woman and a man would have been taken more seriously – but she knew her Bible inside out. Using the Sword of the Spirit she went into battle: 'What I have written to you is no woman's chit-chat, but the word of God; and I write as a member of the Christian Church, against which the gates of Hell cannot prevail.'[14] We often assume other people will take a stand for biblical truth – people who are better qualified or more high profile than us. We might feel we can take a back seat and let others take the flack. Wouldn't it be great if more ordinary Christians, like Argula, armed with a knowledge of God's Word, were prepared to contend for the gospel in the public sphere.

Argula counted the cost of her actions. She fully expected to be martyred:

> *I would dearly like to know what they have to gain if they were to murder me right now ... In the name of God, then, if Christians are to be martyred in this town, just as they were in Jerusalem, may God's will be done as far as I'm concerned ... I am persuaded, too, that if I am given grace to suffer death for his name, many hearts would be awakened. Yes, and whereas I have written on my own, a hundred women would emerge to write against them.[15]*

If she was killed or her property confiscated, she knew she could trust God to care for her young family: 'God will surely care for my four children, and send the birds of the air to feed them and clothe them with the flowers of the field.'[16] How often are we put off from speaking out for Christ, or standing up for biblical truth, because we are worried what the consequences might be? How often are we reluctant to do what we know to be right because it might damage our reputation, our friendships or our finances? Argula stood up for her faith regardless of the consequences, knowing she could entrust her family, her fortune and her future into God's hands.

Knowing her life might be cut short at any time, she made the most of every opportunity. Over the following year Argula wrote other letters to aristocratic contacts to encourage them to consider, or to stand firm for, the gospel. She also used social occasions to witness for Christ. She wrote a thank-you letter to Duke Johann of Simmern for a dinner party she attended. She had obviously used the occasion to witness to him, and then used the letter to encourage him to spread the gospel among the poor in his territories:

> *Noble Prince, gracious Lord, when I was invited by your Princely Grace and some of my other lords to a meal yesterday evening, for which I most humbly thank all concerned, I recognised from several of your Princely Grace's statements that he is beginning to read the Scriptures and the Word of God; and also that your Princely Grace now sees the light, which gives me no little pleasure*

... May your Princely Grace bring his advice and influence to bear, so that the poor are not debarred from the Kingdom of God.[17]

From 1523 to 1524 Argula von Grumbach was at the centre of evangelical activity in Bavaria – then she disappeared. She wrote no more public letters after 1524. Given her refusal to back down even when her life was threatened, it seems unlikely that she stopped writing due to fear of reprisals or family pressure. It seems more likely that with the financial difficulties that followed her husband's job loss she was overwhelmed with the minutiae of everyday life – the ordinary struggle to survive. There is one letter to a Jewish moneylender thanking him for not foreclosing on a loan, which her husband had forgotten to repay. She had to pawn a gold necklace as surety. She remained at home with her family. She took full charge of the children's education, making sure they had Protestant tutors and contact with evangelicals in other parts of Germany. She was also putting up with her husband's 'tyranny', which, given the culture of the time, almost certainly involved physical violence. It seems she struggled to know what a Christian response to such treatment should be. In a poem written in response to a rhyming attack she wrote: 'May God teach me to understand, How to conduct myself towards my man.'[18]

She did have one final foray into public life when, in 1530, she travelled to Augsburg to support the Protestant delegates at the conference to agree a confession of faith for Germany. She even went to meet Luther, who, outlawed by the Holy Roman Emperor, could not risk attending the meeting, so was holed up in Coburg Castle. During their conversation Argula asked Martin to pass on advice on weaning the children to Katie!

Her husband Friedrich died that same year. In many ways it must have been a relief, but it was now her sole responsibility to run the estates, deal with creditors and bring up the children. Although she did remarry in 1533 – her new husband was a man with the delightful name of Poppo von Schlick – he died eighteen months later, leaving her a widow once again. By this time it was clear that Argula's pamphleteering had failed. Far from Bavaria becoming a Protestant state it had become a heartland of the Counter-Reformation – the Roman Catholic backlash against evangelical reform. She thought she would go out in a blaze of glory – gruesomely martyred for the cause – but her martyrdom was much less dramatic – an on-going struggle to live and witness for Christ in a hostile world.

Life as a widow was tough. Male relatives often resented a woman being in charge of family estates – Argula's friend Dorothea von Kluge was bankrupted and physically attacked by members of her own family. In 1542 there was a court case to try and take guardianship of the children away from Argula. Her tenants often refused to pay the rent – assuming that as their 'landlord' was a vulnerable widow they would get away with it. They were wrong! When one tenant threatened and insulted her, because she tried to remove him from a house he had no right to live in, she put him in the stocks.

She kept the guardianship of her children and worked tirelessly to make sure they had a Christian education, although the cost was crippling. As they were from a noble family, the children were sent away to be educated when they were only seven years old. With Bavaria a Catholic state, for most of their schooling they were 100 miles from home in the Protestant enclave of Nuremberg. Their mother had to find money not only for school fees but also for lodgings, books and clothes. The boys' letters not only complain of homesickness, unfamiliar food and teachers but also one begs for a new doublet to replace one that is embarrassingly tight and another asks for advice on how to darn shabby clothes. Once they moved on to 'finishing school' at court, Argula had to find even more money to pay for servants to wait on them.

Even though it was culturally expected, she found it hard to have her children so far from home. She made sure that their teachers were godly men. As pupils usually lodged with teachers and their families, it was important that they were morally and theologically upright. Generally they seem to have done a good job, but, like typical teenagers, the boys' behaviour sometimes left a lot to be desired. One tutor sent this report about George: 'If he is to continue as my pupil he will have to eat humble pie like everyone else, so that the evil he is so full of can be punished. If he doesn't learn this in his youth he will be a slave to evil in his maturity and reveal his lack of self-knowledge.'[19] Despite the best efforts of Argula and the teachers, it was not always possible to stop the boys from being influenced by the behaviour of other students, who habitually fought, drank excessively and visited prostitutes. George was wounded in a brawl in 1533, never fully recovered and died in 1539. Gottfried caused fewer worries. He was a hardworking boy, who seems to have been a committed Christian from an early age. He wrote to his mother, 'I am really working hard at my studies and you should have no doubt about it that if God gives me grace I will ensure that I grow up to be a good person, even if my brother does not turn out so well.'[20] That particular brother was Hans-Georg. Despite his younger brother's attempts to keep him on the straight and narrow, Hans-Georg was a cause of constant anxiety to his mother. She wrote to him, 'I go on lamenting in my prayers to God that the children I have borne and nourished at my breast and raised with such great worry, cost and anxiety have proved so disobedient.'[21] One letter implies that this time he really had over-stepped the mark – there are few details, but there appears to have been a real scandal: 'I was terribly shocked to hear about what happened at Burggrumbach from your letter and before that from [other] people ... God grant that you may repent and improve in the future ... And on your life see that you tell no one anything about it, trust no one and keep the matter absolutely secret.'[22] It doesn't seem that he did 'repent and improve'. Hans-Georg was murdered in 1543.

Her absent children's behaviour was not the only thing for Argula to worry about. In an age when a third of children died under the age of five, with small pox, plague and infection endemic and most medicine little more than quackery, any illness was to be feared. The doctor advised Gottfried to cut out cheese to cure his headaches. Apparently it worked. Headaches were one thing – the plague was another thing altogether. In 1532 her daughter Appolonia was ill with the plague in Nuremberg for fifty-one weeks! She was lucky to survive. Her mother wrote to her, 'My dear daughter ...I am so delighted you have taken a turn for the better ... that the spots and pustules have disappeared ... so follow the advice of your doctor and be grateful to God and to him; be godfearing, honest, patient and good ...'[23] Although she recovered from this illness,

Appolonia died in 1539, the same year as her brother George, when she was still relatively young.

Sending her children away to school was the only option if they were to receive a Christian education. The treatment of Arsacius Seehofer at Ingolstadt University highlighted the danger for Protestant students in Bavaria. Although Argula's decision to send them to Nuremberg and elsewhere had mixed results, they at least had the opportunity to be taught by some of the best evangelical tutors and avoided being persecuted for their faith. When their father was alive, it probably made sense for them to be away from his anti-Christian influence. After his death Argula appreciated that her sons had godly male role models. Gottfried and Appolonia shared their mother's faith. George and Hans-Georg did not. In a very difficult situation she did the best she could.

Although family and business concerns took up a lot of her time, she was determined to make the most of every opportunity to spread the gospel and build up believers in Bavaria. In the early 1520s, when she was one of the most famous women in Germany, it must have seemed that anything was possible. Luther's ideas were spreading throughout Europe and, despite some setbacks, many assumed that eventually Protestantism would triumph everywhere. In many areas it did – but not in Argula's Bavaria. The opposition to Seehofer and to her own pamphlet campaign hardened into aggressive and triumphalist Catholicism, which made life very difficult for evangelicals. It would have been easy for Argula to be despondent, give up and just live a quiet life on her estates, but she didn't. She continued to be in contact with the leaders of the Reformation elsewhere in Germany, particularly Osiander in Nuremberg. She acquired and distributed evangelical pamphlets from Luther's Wittenberg, despite the risks, and encouraged the minister on one of her estates to preach from the Bible. There is a still a Lutheran church there today – dating from Argula's time. It was clear that there was now no point writing to encourage the Bavarian nobility to embrace reform – their actions made it very clear they would not – but Argula did try to use her influence in other areas. When she visited a relative who was a canon living in the town of Zeilitzhaim, she tried to win him over with gifts of cheese and wine. She used her stays as an excuse to encourage an evangelical canon in the same town. He appreciated her fellowship and partnership in the gospel. He wrote saying, 'When her ladyship comes, I hope to be able to transform matters with her help.'[24] She built up a network of friends who supported and encouraged each other pastorally and practically. The city clerk of Wurzburg wrote to her as his 'Dear sister in Christ'. They exchanged pamphlets and he helped her supervise her vineyards. She sent gifts and wrote letters to evangelical friends who needed support. She gave a cask of wine and a kind letter to a friend whose child had died, encouraging her to trust in Christ. Having been in the spotlight, when such public activities became impossible, she went under the radar. She adapted to circumstances and never gave up.

Argula ended her life in obscurity, and the exact details of her death are unknown. In 1586 it was reported that she had died in 1554. That is possible – but it is also possible that she died much later. In 1563 court records show that the Duke of Bavaria imprisoned 'the old Staufferin' for circulating anti-Catholic books. This may have been another member of the von Stauff family, but it sounds like just the kind of thing that Argula would get up to. The Council encouraged the Duke to be lenient: 'The Staufferin is an enfeebled old lady. Better to have pity on her age and stupidity.'[25] By this date Argula would have been seventy-one. It makes sense to think that in her old age she was still contending and taking risks for the gospel.

The Bible often talks of the Christian life being a struggle – even a battle – but so often we opt out of the fight and take the course of least resistance. Argula von Grumbach was a gospel warrior. She was prepared to fight for Christ, whatever the cost. Initially that fight was public and dramatic; later it was private but still persistent. Historically speaking her stand looks futile as anti-Protestant forces took control in Bavaria; personally she may have felt a failure as her sons abandoned her faith; but in God's eyes she was one armed with the 'full armour of God, so that when the day of evil comes, you may be able to stand your ground, and after you have done everything, to stand'.[26]

BIBLE STUDY & REFLECTION

Ephesians 6:10–21

1. In what ways would Argula have been more aware that she was in a spiritual battle than we might be?

2. Why would it have been particularly hard for her to 'stand firm' (v. 14)?

3. When do you find it hardest to stand firm for Christ?

4. How did Argula show that she was dressed for battle:

   • with her 'feet fitted with the readiness that comes from the gospel of peace' (v. 15)?
   • with the 'shield of faith' (v. 16)?
   • with the 'helmet of salvation' (v. 17)?
   • with the 'sword of the Spirit' (v. 17)?

5. How can we make sure we are ready for battle in the same way?

6. Paul here asks for prayer that he would proclaim the gospel fearlessly in all circumstances (v. 19). In what different circumstances was Argula able to proclaim the gospel?

7. What opportunities do you have?

8. Pray for courage and clarity as you take a fearless stand for Christ (vv. 19–20)!

CHAPTER FOUR

Katharina Zell
1498–1562
A Compassionate Co-worker

What does love look like? The word has now come to be associated with soppy sentimentalism — hearts, roses and cards with cute puppies. In church circles love and clear biblical teaching can be set against each other. Emphasising love over doctrine is often an excuse for avoiding difficult Bible truths. Emphasising doctrine over love can lead to a harsh biblicism that is very off-putting. What does real biblical love look like in practice? Although Katharina Zell made mistakes, as we all do, she was determined to live a life that glorified God by loving him with all her heart, soul, mind and strength and by loving her neighbour as herself. Her radical life challenged others, and she was not always popular. At times she did not live up to her own high standards, but that an ordinary woman could achieve so much, and care so deeply for those around her, must surely challenge us to live lives that reflect the Lord Jesus more closely.

Katharina Schutz was born in Strasbourg, then in Germany, around 1498. It was quite a large town for the time, with about 20,000 inhabitants. It was an exciting place to grow up. It was a trade centre and a base of the new printing industry, so new ideas could be circulated and discussed. Her family was not wealthy – her father was a woodworker – but there was always enough food on the table, and when her sisters married, there was money spare for a decent dowry. She was the fifth of ten children – six girls and four boys. Her family seems to have been close and supportive, and her parents taught even the girls to read and write in German and encouraged the children to think for themselves.

Katharina was a very devout little girl. When she was only ten, she dedicated her life to the church. She never wanted to be a nun, but assumed that to please God she would have to be celibate. As she would never marry, and in order not to be a burden to her family, she trained as a tapestry weaver. She did everything a girl could do to get in God's good books. She went to Mass, prayed to the saints, cared for the poor and was devoted to the Virgin Mary. She read tracts criticising the abuses of the Catholic Church — the immorality and greed of many priests was common knowledge — and agreed that the solution was to demand higher standards of behaviour. Her own standards were unattainably high, yet however hard she tried she could never be confident that she had done enough to please God. Years later she wrote, 'Since, however, my distress about the Kingdom of Heaven grew great and in all my hard works, worship, and great pain of body I could not find or obtain from all the clergy any comfort or certainty of the love and grace of God, I became weak and sick to death in soul and body.'[1]

Just as Katharina was becoming desperate in her quest for peace with God, things began to change in Strasbourg. Katharina was not alone in needing help. Some were demanding more from the clergy. In 1516 the priest at the Cathedral Church was removed from office, considered unfit to preach. There were strange spiritual outpourings. In 1518 Strasbourg was struck by a 'dancing plague'. Over 400 people danced manically in the streets, apparently inspired by St Vitus, leading to deaths from exhaustion and heart attacks. The city was ready for the gospel!

In 1518, when Strasbourg was still recovering from St Vitus' dance, Matthias Zell arrived as the priest of St Lawrence Church. Luther's ninety-five theses had only been published the year before, but already Zell seemed positive about reform. Part of his job involved hearing confession on behalf of the bishop for all sorts of minor misdemeanours, such as women not being purified after childbirth. This involved payment to the church for the ceremony, even if there had been a miscarriage or stillbirth. Zell should have excommunicated the women – he didn't! As Luther's writings were being read by his parishioners, Zell felt he should read them too. He was impressed and his preaching became more and more biblical and gospel focused. He emphasised the authority of the Bible over that of the Church. He taught that salvation could only be found in the death of Christ and that all believers had equal access to God and equal value in his sight. The people of Strasbourg flocked to hear him preach.

As a member of his congregation Katharina was also pointed towards Luther's works. Her life was transformed:

> *Then God had mercy on us and many people. He awakened and sent out by tongue and writings the dear and now blessed Dr Martin Luther,*

who described the Lord Jesus Christ for me and others in such a lovely way that I thought I had been drawn out of the depths of the earth, yes out of grim bitter hell, into the sweet lovely kingdom of heaven.[2]

Katharina became even more determined to dedicate her life to God. Although at times throughout her life she struggled to have assurance of her salvation, she now wanted to serve Christ in response to his love for her rather than to try and earn his favour. She was also determined to live her life under the authority of the Bible rather than the teachings of the Church. This had some unexpected consequences for her life.

In 1523 Matthias and Katharina decided they should get married. She was twenty-five, he was twenty years older. Zell was not the first priest in the town to get married, but he was the most influential, and Katharina was unusual as she was a respectable woman from an old Strasbourg family rather than an ex-nun or priest's mistress. It was a risky business as the Reformation had not yet been securely established in Strasbourg and all of the seven married priests faced excommunication.

Almost immediately rumours began circulating about the couple. Some were blatantly untrue. It was rumoured that Zell had hanged himself out of remorse

– but he could still be seen alive around town! Others were more believable: he beat her; she had run away; he was having an affair with the serving girl. Matthias thought the rumours were beneath contempt, but Katharina was more aware of the damage being done to the cause of the gospel as she overheard the gossip in the market-place. She was determined to fight back. As she wrote in her public defence of their marriage, 'Silence is half a confession that the lies are true.'[3] She refuted the lies one by one: 'I have never had a maid. I have had the help only of a little girl, too young for that kind of thing, and as for thrashing me, my husband and I have never had an unpleasant 15 minutes.'[4]

From the start Katharina was determined that their marriage would be a partnership for the gospel. She was her husband's social and intellectual equal and she believed that she should be able to work beside him in ministry. She supported Matthias in his increasingly busy schedule. As the Reformation took hold in Strasbourg, services that had just involved reciting the liturgy of the Mass now demanded prepared biblical sermons. From 1526 there were three services each day, with the first at 4 a.m. in summer and 5 a.m. in winter! On Sunday there was a lie-in as the service began at 7 a.m. This service lasted several hours, and then, after a quick bite to eat, there was the mid-day sermon followed by a catechetical service to teach and train new believers and a further service later in the afternoon.

Zell was the most popular preacher in Zurich – often preaching to 3,000 at a time – and predictably this made others jealous. He was criticised for 'dumbing down' the message, but people loved his teaching as they could actually understand what he was saying, unlike with some of the more intellectual preachers. Katharina kept his feet firmly on the ground as, through her pastoral visits and chatting with parishioners in the market-place, she helped him understand the needs of ordinary people.

Matthias valued her help, and encouraged her in her own ministry. After his death she wrote,

> *My husband denied me nothing. He did not rule over or compel my faith; he also never put any obstacle in the way of my faith but rather much more he actively furthered and helped me. He granted and allowed me space and will to read, hear, pray, study, and be active in all good things, early and late, day and night: indeed, he took great joy in that – even when it meant less attention to or neglect in looking after his physical needs and running his household.[5]*

For a husband today to put his wife's spiritual growth ahead of a hot dinner and a tidy house is commendable – in the sixteenth century it was extraordinary. Both the Zells were more concerned to live by biblical than social norms. While twenty-first- and sixteenth-century culture praises Marthas, they both knew that it was Mary that Jesus praised.[6]

Katharina also shocked the society of the time by repeatedly doing things that women were not supposed to do. She was remarkable in that, as far as possible, she made sure she built her life on what the Bible said rather than on what contemporary culture said a woman could or could not do – the biblical model was far more liberating! Her public letter in defence of her marriage was not her only published work. Throughout her life she wrote when she felt the situation demanded it. Soon after she was married, when the Protestant men of the nearby town of Kentzingen were sent into exile, she wrote a public letter to encourage their wives to stand firm for Christ. Women were not supposed to write, but she saw no biblical reason why she shouldn't. She wrote, 'I do not seek to be heard as if I were Elizabeth, or John the Baptist, or Nathan the prophet who pointed out his sin to David, or as any of the prophets, but only as the donkey whom the false prophet Balaam heard.'[7]

Women were also not supposed to get involved in public life. Katharina virtually single-handedly reorganised the city's welfare system. In reformed Strasbourg, monasteries no longer had a role to play in caring for the poor and begging for alms was frowned upon. With a growing population, failing harvests and more and more refugees fleeing to the city from Catholic persecution, something had to be done. When 3,000 hungry survivors arrived in Strasbourg following the end of the Peasants' War in 1525, Katharina stepped in to co-ordinate poor relief, and to ensure everybody had food and shelter. She knew that the gospel required her to love her neighbour whatever the cost. It was a huge task, which could only have been achieved by someone with a forceful personality. Her husband's colleague Martin Bucer commented, 'She is a trifle imperious.'[8] She also visited and monitored the 'hospitals' caring for the long-term sick, and when she discovered financial mismanagement, she proposed a series of administrative reforms that were largely adopted by the city council.

Her ideas were taken seriously by the council, and perhaps more surprisingly by her husband's reformed colleagues, who 'never withheld from me their conversation about holy matters and they gladly (from the heart) heard mine'.[9] Katharina was at the centre of the key theological discussions of the day. The city clergy met at their home to discuss their reaction to Anabaptism.[10] Zwingli and Oecolampadius stayed in their home for two weeks when they were on their way to Marburg to debate the doctrine of the Lord's Supper with the Lutherans. Although undoubtedly she contributed to the discussions, she also had to play a more conventional role. She commented, 'For 14 days I was their cook and maid.'[11]

The Zells differed from many of the reformers as they were more tolerant of those with minor theological differences. Zell wrote, 'Anyone who acknowledges Christ as the true Son of God and the sole Saviour of mankind is welcome at my board.'[12] Bucer blamed Katharina's influence! If Katharina's love of neighbour compelled her to social action, her love for God compelled her to love his people – whatever name they were called by. As she explained,

> *Luther, Zwingli, Schwenckfeld and all good teachers and preachers, together with the prophets and apostles, did not become a sacrifice on the cross for me, but Christ the Son of God Himself ... I also do not want to be called after them or by their names, but only to be called a Christian, after my only Lord and Master Christ.*[13]

Katharina once again was more concerned to follow the Bible than the Christian culture in Strasbourg. She felt that the Bible taught that a Christian was anyone who trusted in the death of the Lord Jesus alone for their salvation. When she felt that some evangelical leaders were in danger of adding extra qualifications to this definition, she spoke out. Katharina wrote to

Luther encouraging him to bury his differences with those who disagreed with him on what Katharina saw as the secondary issue of Holy Communion, in the name of Christian love. Luther took over a year to reply, and when he did, he replied firmly that for him Communion was not a secondary issue!

Unfortunately it can also be true today that those who claim to hold to the reformers' doctrine of justification by faith alone subtly appear to add other conditions if someone is to be a 'proper' Christian. A correct emphasis on theological accuracy can lead to the kind of judgementalism that Katharina encountered and that excludes those who don't agree on even the tiniest doctrinal points. Katharina cared about doctrine, but she also cared for God's people even if they disagreed on some issues.

The Zells put their theological views into practice by welcoming anyone in need of hospitality. Katharina wrote, 'What did their names matter to us? We were not obliged to share the ideas and faith of anyone, but were obligated to show to each one love, service, and mercy as our teacher Christ has taught us.'[14] When the 150 men of Kenzingen fled to Strasbourg in 1524, Katharina put eighty of them up in the parsonage for four weeks! A few years later fifteen evangelical clergy arrived from Baden when the prince imposed Catholicism in the area. One of them, who had four small children, ended up spending the whole winter with the Zells. They befriended all who called themselves Christians – which at times caused them problems. Caspar Schwenckfeld, a nobleman who had become a Protestant, came to stay for a year or so. Gradually his views became less and less orthodox, and they struggled to maintain their friendship while distancing themselves from his ideas. As time went on this relationship was to cause Katharina real difficulty.

On the surface Katharina appears to have been a forceful and independent woman, determined to live a biblically acceptable rather than a socially acceptable life. She pushed the boundaries of what was appropriate behaviour for a Christian woman. Although she believed that the Bible taught that ordination, leadership and preaching were male roles, all other areas of ministry were open to her – but when she got married, she would never have expected to have been effectively Matthias' assistant minister. They longed for a family, and Katharina looked forward to teaching and training her own children to love the Lord Jesus. Tragically she never had the opportunity as the couple's two children both died when they were very young. She was overwhelmed with grief and was tempted to see her loss as a punishment from God, whom she felt she must have displeased in some way. Speaking at Matthias' funeral, years later, Katharina remembered her children:

I hope to obtain and see that resurrection with my dear husband, along with our dear children. (Together we had two, and they lie in this place.) It is now in the twenty-first year since with great pain! we carried out our first child and trod this place with him; he was the first person buried in this graveyard, where with such fitting earnestness he [Zell] so often longed to come.[15]

Their first child died in 1527, the second probably in 1531. 1531 was a bad year. In April Katharina was so ill, perhaps following childbirth, that Matthias thought she was dying. In October they heard the dreadful news of Zwingli's death at the Battle of Kappel. In November there was an outbreak of plague in Strasbourg in which several friends died. Although Katharina was still recovering from serious illness herself, she risked infection by caring for her friends Wolfgang and Agnes Capito. When Agnes died, she helped the barely house-trained Capito with the housework until Bucer found him a suitable new wife.[16]

Grief at the loss of her children motivated her to work even harder than she had before. It would have been easy for her to have retreated from public life and to have avoided women who had been blessed with children – but this is far from what she did. Her suffering gave her more understanding of those she cared for, and her writings gained pastoral depth. Although she would not be able to teach her own children about Jesus, she could help other mothers. She edited a hymn-book and added simple folk tunes, hoping that parents would use it to teach their children rather than leading them astray. It seems that the popular songs of the sixteenth century were no more suitable for children than are the songs of today. Katharina imagines a parent saying, 'Up till now we have all sung bad songs, to the scandal of our souls and our neighbours' souls.'[17] With the new hymn-book they would have more suitable songs to sing, as Katharina explains: 'A poor mother would so gladly sleep, but at midnight she must rock the wailing baby and sing it a song about godly things.'[18] A meditation on the Lord's Prayer, originally planned for her own children, was also eventually published and dedicated to the women of a neighbouring city.

Similarly Katharina made the most of the time and opportunities available to her as a woman without children. She was able to join her husband when he visited other centres of reform. In 1538 she travelled through Switzerland, to Constance, Swabia, Nurnberg and Wittenberg, where they stayed with the Luthers. Capito warned Luther about Katharina: 'If the planned trip comes about you will clearly hear that our women are not all silent. But she is good and devout.'[19] Katharina also became more involved in reconciling squabbling reformers. Together the Zells mediated in disagreements over whether a chalice should be made of silver or gold, and whether wafers or bread should be used at the Lord's Supper. Where the Bible was unclear, they encouraged compromise and understanding. During Calvin's time in Strasbourg – when he was temporarily thrown out of Geneva – he became enraged by the Strasbourg ministers' decision to back a preacher he considered heretical. Bucer called on the Zells to calm him down!

Matthias was twenty years older than Katharina. As he grew older, he needed more help from his wife. He continued to preach daily to the last. Eventually he died in 1548, when he was seventy and Katharina only fifty years old. She was heart-broken. Bucer preached at the funeral, and afterwards, once again breaking with convention, Katharina gave a eulogy. She had not planned to speak, but she felt she had to encourage the congregation to honour her husband's memory. Although some have seen her speech as the act of a feminist pioneer, it was not controversial at the time. It was seen as what it was – the spontaneous reaction of a grieving widow: 'But with what great pain of heart I lose our companionship and lament to God that He has exacted this of me so quickly and made me an afflicted widow! [My husband's] death is so unbearable to me, speaking from the view point of my flesh: I will mourn it to my grave.'[20]

After the funeral Katharina collapsed and seems to have suffered a nervous breakdown. Bucer was worried about her and encouraged her to stay with friends in Basel. He wrote on her behalf:

> *The widow of our Zell, a godly and saintly woman, comes to you that perchance she may find some solace for her grief. She is human. How does the heavenly Father humble those endowed with the greatest gifts! Her zeal is incredible for Christ's lowliest and afflicted. She knows and searches the mysteries of Christ. Because she is resentful of their dispensation she heaps upon herself frightful reproaches. She is all too human. Truly this is a trial from the Lord and it is astounding. Comfort her patiently for the love of her husband, a sincere and faithful servant of Christ ...*[21]

Although Katharina's health improved, she found life without Matthias very hard. She missed him. She wrote to Schwenckfeld, who despite their differences remained a friend, 'He much loved me and held me in great honor (not because of my beauty or wealth: I never had much of either) but because of my zeal, deeds, and faith, which were all he sought for in me at the beginning of our marriage. I was never worthy of this love and honour.'[22]

No longer the wife of a respected spiritual leader, she felt her loss of status and opportunities for ministry: 'I am now a poor solitary woman, fit only (as some say) to spin or wait on the sick.'[23] Politically life was more difficult too. In an attempt to restore religious peace the Holy Roman Emperor had insisted on an Interim Agreement.[24] The Mass was reinstated in some churches, there were to be no more clerical marriages and the leaders of the Reformation in Strasbourg had to go into exile. Life was very insecure. She also found herself caught up in the middle of a theological controversy. As she refused to distance herself from her friend Schwenckfeld, she was labelled a heretic. She had always hated labels and intolerance and would not stand with the increasingly hardline Strasbourg ministers or with the increasingly radical Schwenckfeld. Rabus, Zell's successor as minister in Strasbourg, launched a vitriolic attack on Katharina. When she finally wrote to object, he poured scorn on her 'poisonous, envious, lying writing'.[25] His attitude was particularly painful as he had lived with the Zells as a young man and had called her his foster-mother. The only label she would use for herself was 'Christian'. She was demonised by both sides, but stuck to her guns: 'I will demonstrate my love and service everywhere to whoever seeks it, but I will not give myself as a prisoner to anyone.'[26]

Despite her difficulties she did indeed 'demonstrate [her] love and service everywhere to whoever seeks it'.

She was allowed to continue living in the church house for over two years after her husband's death and she used it as she had always done: 'I have been allowed to keep the parsonage which belongs to the parish. I take in anyone who comes. It is always full.'[27] Bucer took advantage of her hospitality when he missed the Interim deadline for going into exile. She hid him for three weeks before he left for the safety of England. He left two gold pieces to thank her. She would not take them!

> *You put me to shame to think that you would leave money for me, as if I would take a heller from you poor pilgrims and my revered ministers. I wish I could have done better for you but my Matthew has taken all my gaiety with him. I intended to return the two gold pieces with this letter … but a refugee minister has just come in with five children, and the wife of another who saw her husband beheaded before her eyes. I divided the one gold piece between them as a present. The other I enclose. You will need it.[28]*

She continued to care for all those who needed her help in spite of her own problems. In particular she looked after two people whom the rest of the city was happy to ignore. The first was her nephew, who suffered from syphilis. Syphilis had arrived in Europe from America after Columbus' discovery of the New World. As it was a sexually transmitted disease, sufferers were ostracised. The symptoms were terrifying and there was no cure. When Katharina visited her nephew in hospital, she was horrified by the conditions. After complaining to the authorities, she brought him home to care for him herself. It was a full-time job. Some criticised her for irregular attendance at church. She replied, 'I wish that you preachers with your wives and "gracious ladies" together with many hypocritical people who attend sermons, sometimes had to do what I sometimes must do during sermon time! To undertake such great work and horror, to wash filth and urine night and day, so that I use up all of my strength.'[29]

She also cared for Felix Armbruster, who suffered from the other untouchable disease – leprosy. Although he had been an eminent citizen of Strasbourg, his illness forced him to live outside the city walls. He was a widower and his only daughter refused to see him. Only Katharina cared. She visited when she could, and when her nephew's demands and her own poor health made that impossible, she wrote to him. In particular she wrote him meditations on the psalms to comfort him in his loneliness. Her suffering had made her even more compassionate. She had always cared, now she understood as well. She wrote to him, 'My dear Sir Felix, you and I have talked together in many conversations about the way things stand between God and ourselves and how He has so severely visited you.'[30]

Despite all Katharina and Matthias had done for the city, the people of Strasbourg abandoned her when she needed them most. Matthias had warned her just before his death that this would be the case. Katharina noted that his predictions 'have already in part come true. I am as little valued by our clergy as if I had never served the church'.[31] Despite their differences, the first generation of reformers in Strasbourg had united around the gospel. They shared personal experiences of freedom in Christ and developed close friendships. Three decades after the Reformation began the landscape was changing. Katharina's love for her neighbour, whatever their disagreements on minor issues, was no longer acceptable. Although everything she did had solid biblical foundations, she didn't fit the new mould. She was expected to take sides – she refused. Things came to a head shortly before she died. Two of her female friends, who had been followers of Schwenckfeld, died. Their families were aware that if any of the city ministers conducted the funerals, they would take the opportunity to criticise their faith – but the women had to be decently buried. Katharina offered to help. She was elderly and so unwell that she had to be carried to the graveside, but she read out the funeral service for her friends. The authorities were furious and planned to reprimand her publically when she was well enough. She escaped that final humiliation by dying soon afterwards.

Given the circumstances her own funeral was always going to be controversial as well. Now having 'proof' that she was a Schwenckfelder, the city clergy refused to bury her too. Eventually, for old times' sake, Bucer's former secretary agreed to take the service. Despite Katharina's age, increasing isolation and the disapproval of the powers that be, over 200 townspeople attended.

When she was a young woman, Katharina had worked tirelessly, if fruitlessly, to live a life good enough to earn God's approval. When she finally understood the gospel of grace, her life was transformed. Having been forgiven and accepted by God through Christ's death on her behalf, she was set free to live to please Him. As she read and applied the Bible day by day, she could see what her life as a Christian woman might look like. If what society or even church leaders said disagreed with what the Bible taught, she went with the Bible. Not surprisingly this meant she lived a life that was far more radical and liberated than the social norms of the time allowed. She was blessed with a loving and supportive husband, who gave her space to use her many gifts in Christ's service as together they showed Christ's compassion to all who trusted in Him. Katharina's life challenges us today to model our lives on what the Bible says rather than what our culture — even our Christian culture — expects.

BIBLE STUDY & REFLECTION

Titus 2:3–5; 3:3–11

1. How might Christian women today be tempted to model themselves (a) on the world and (b) on Christian culture rather than on what the Bible teaches? How was this the same or different in Katharina's day?

2. What impact did learning that 'he saved us, not because of righteous things we had done, but because of his mercy' (3:5) have on Katharina's life?

3. 3:7–8 argues that being justified by grace will lead to a devotion to 'doing what is good'. How was that shown in Katharina's life?

4. Is that true of your life?

5. How did Katharina and her husband put 3:9–11 into practice?

6. What 'foolish controversies' might you be tempted to indulge in? How might Katharina's example be helpful?

7. How far did Katharina live up to the model in 2:3–5 in her:
   • general lifestyle (vv. 3,5)?
   • writings (v. 4)?
   • attitude to others (v. 5)?

8. If you are an older (!) woman, how can you model the biblical role of women more effectively?

9. If you are a younger woman, how far are you willing to learn from others and to put the teaching of verses 4 to 5 into practice?

CHAPTER FIVE

Wibrandis Rosenblatt
1504–1564
A Wonderful Wife

I magine the scene – a smart event, with everybody dressed up to the nines. An impressive-looking woman approaches and asks, 'What do you do?' 'Oh, I'm just a mum' is barely heard before she moves on to find someone more interesting to talk to. Being a wife and mother comes pretty low in the pecking order for a twenty-first-century woman. Surely only someone with no self-esteem, skills or ambition could put up with looking after screaming kids all day? Wibrandis Rosenblatt was only ever a wife and mother – to four husbands and hoards of children and step-children – but the role she played in the Reformation was undeniable. Her gifts may have been far less spectacular than those of Katharina Zell, but they were perfect for the situation in which she found herself. I hope her story will help us to realise that often being 'just a mum' can be the most important job of all.

Wibrandis was born just east of Basel, in Switzerland, in 1504. Her name was unusual even for the time. In the year she was born three women who were buried locally were made saints – the stories on which their sanctity rested were probably made up, but they became local celebrities. Wibrandis' parents decided to name her after one of them. The other two were called Kunegundis and Mechtundis – so Wibrandis got off relatively lightly. Her father was a respected citizen. When Wibrandis was six, he became mayor of their town and he was also knighted for bravery in the emperor's military campaigns. He was often away fighting, so the family – Wibrandis, her mother and brother Adelberg – moved to Basel to be nearer relatives. They stayed put even after Wibrandis' father was given an estate in Austria by the grateful emperor. They far preferred the bustle of Basel to the more formal, rural life of the minor aristocracy.

In 1524, when she was twenty, Wibrandis married for the first time. Her husband was Ludwig Keller – or Cellarius, as he liked to call himself. He would have been quite a good catch. He was a humanist scholar, who, although sympathetic to the new evangelical movement, never actively pushed for reform. The couple had one daughter – also called Wibrandis – before Keller died in 1526, after just two years of marriage. Wibrandis was a widow at twenty-two.

Early deaths from disease and accidents were common in the sixteenth century and remarriage usually followed quite quickly. Widows needed the protection only marriage could offer and men needed someone to look after their home and mother-less children. That Wibrandis was married again within two years would not have been thought strange. The fact that she married a priest twenty years older than her without the support of her parents was shocking.

Wibrandis had somehow come to trust in Christ over those two years, presumably by hearing the gospel from one of the evangelical preachers who were becoming increasingly influential in Basel. Possibly she attended Oecolampadius' lectures on the Bible, which attracted not only students from the university but also over 400 townspeople. Whatever happened, by 1528 she was an established member of the Protestant community in the city. She was a well brought up, respectable

Christian widow – the perfect match for one of the reforming priests who now felt free to marry.

Oecolampadius' friends felt that he needed a wife. His mother, who had acted as his housekeeper, died in February 1528. His colleague Capito, who had recently married himself, wrote suggesting that now was the perfect time to marry – as long as the wife shared his faith and would support him in ministry. As he put it, 'I would prefer the burden of celibacy over the yoke of an unequal marriage, and it will be unequal, I think, if you marry a woman who is not sincerely and truly a Christian, that is, who is not self-denying.'[1] Oecolampadius replied, 'Don't worry about my marrying. I appreciate your concern. Either I shall find a Christian sister ... or I will remain unmarried. Such a woman is a rare bird, but perhaps one can be netted. I cannot stand my present housekeeper. I wouldn't for a moment consider marrying her.'[2] One complaint against the housekeeper was that she was slandering a widow of good reputation. It seems likely that Wibrandis was already on the scene, and that the housekeeper was trying to remove the competition. Nevertheless, within weeks Oecolampadius and Wibrandis were married. He was forty-five – she was twenty-four. One observer wrote a less than flattering description of the couple: 'A decrepit old man with trembling head and body, so emaciated and wasted that you might call him a living corpse, has married an elegant and blooming girl of 20, more or less.'[3] The age gap was not the only issue. Some members of her family were horrified that she was marrying a priest. Oecolampadius wrote to Zwingli, 'Pray to the Lord, that it may be blessed and redound to his glory; the woman has many prominent foes as well as friends of the gospel in her family.'[4]

It wasn't a love match – few marriages in those days were expected to be – but it was an effective partnership. Oecolampadius wrote to Capito, 'My wife is what I always wanted and I wish for no other. She is not contentious, garrulous, or a gadabout, but looks after the household. She is too simple to be proud and too discreet to be condemned.'[5] Wibrandis was more than just a housekeeper. A little more than nine months after the wedding, on Christmas Eve 1528, their son, Eusebius, was born. Wibrandis was content with her lot. She made friends with other ministers' wives – Capito's wife, Agnes, gave her a prayer book as a present, and she made cheese for the Bucer family. The couple bought a vineyard outside the city, where the family spent autumn holidays harvesting the grapes. Although he was very serious and hardworking, Oecolampadius was a godly and sensitive husband. Calvin commented on his meekness; Luther described him as 'liberal, prudent and Christian';[6] and Capito called him 'this most saintly man'.[7] Life was good.

However, as we have seen, peaceful family times were not the norm if you were the wife of a reformer. Soon after Eusebius was born, all hell broke loose in Basel – and Oecolampadius was largely to blame! He may have been personally meek and saintly, but his attitude to reform was uncompromising. He, and the other reforming ministers, demanded an end to celebrations of the Mass, the removal of all pictures and statues of saints from churches, and the expulsion of all Roman Catholic members of the town council. As the council hesitated, rioters roamed the streets smashing 'blasphemous' images, and a mob, a thousand strong, ransacked the cathedral. The council capitulated. Reform was established in Basel and Oecolampadius was installed as minister of the cathedral. The problems did not end there, though. Not surprisingly there was ongoing conflict with the town council, which Oecolampadius had to deal with on a daily basis – issues of church discipline, church property and what to do with the Anabaptists.[8]

Wibrandis was unfazed by the chaos. She created a haven for the family that her exhausted and stressed husband could retreat to. He enjoyed coming home – to the humdrum domestic worries that could take his mind off politics and theology. He loved spending time with Eusebius, who was 'a gentle and quiet child unless hungry, thirsty or in need of a change', although he worried about his health: 'He is very subject to colds and coughing. I fear he will not live long.'[9] Two more children, both girls, were born in the next two years – Irene and Aletheia. Wibrandis also had to care for her widowed mother and her little daughter from her first marriage. That would be plenty for most women to cope with, but as the wife of a prominent minister, Wibrandis was also expected to house and entertain eminent visitors to Basel – Zwingli, Bucer and Capito, as well as the heretic Servetus, who would later be burned at the stake in Calvin's Geneva. Wibrandis appears to have coped effortlessly with whatever challenges faced her. She had found her niche, and she probably expected life to continue in much the same way for many years to come.

Unfortunately, after under four years of marriage, her settled life came to an end. Initially it looked as though change might take the form of a move – which would have been traumatic enough for a woman who had spent almost all her life in Basel. After Zwingli's death, Oecolampadius was asked to replace him as minister in Zurich – a tough posting given the dramatic defeat of Zwingli and the Zurich Protestants at the Battle of Kappel. The move never happened as Oecolampadius was too ill to travel. He was suffering from an ulcer, which led to septicaemia. He knew he was dying and passed Eusebius, Irene and Aletheia into Wibrandis' care, reminding her of the meanings of the Greek names they had given the children: 'Take care that they become what is suggested by their names: pious, peace-loving, and truthful.'[10] Just a couple of months after the death of Zwingli, Oecolampadius too was dead. To blacken his name his enemies said he had committed suicide, but the vast numbers at his funeral showed that few believed the rumours – although Luther is said to have done so! Despite the problems Basel had experienced under his influence, the city appreciated all Oecolampadius had done to bring about reform.

The future looked bleak for Wibrandis. She had four small children to care for and no means of support, but her reputation saved her. Her Christian character, her competence in household management and her care for Oecolampadius and the children was well known in Basel and beyond. She had been married twice to very different men in very different circumstances, and had shown that she was adaptable and capable. She would not be on the shelf for long.

Capito's beloved wife, Agnes, had died shortly before Oecolampadius. He was heart-broken and contemplated suicide:

> *My dear sister and wife Agnes, my loyal helper in all services to God, was sick and died during those same days. She died peacefully, quietly and in full devotion to God, but her death did not fail to elicit great disquiet and grief from me ... for several days, I and others were able to contemplate nothing else*

but that God would want to put an end to my existence and take me from this earth as well.'[11]

His friends were worried about him. He was undomesticated, volatile and a financial disaster area. He was also a romantic, who was quite likely to fall in love with someone unsuitable. Bucer – the arch matchmaker – went into action. He thought Wibrandis would be the ideal candidate, but Capito wanted to marry the widow of Augustin Bader. Her husband had been executed for setting himself up as an Anabaptist[12] king and declaring that his infant son was the messiah! Bucer wrote to his friend Ambrose Blaurer,

My choice for Capito is the widow of Oecolampadius, but he inclines to Sabina Bader, the widow of the Anabaptist king. She may have been innocent of her husband's designs, but she was the queen, and such a marriage will hurt the evangelical churches. Besides Capito is so mercurial that he needs a demure and not a domineering wife. I thought first of our Margareta [Blaurer's sister], but he cooks up such fantastic schemes, which do him no good and embarrass others, that I think she would be of more service unencumbered by him ... Capito puts love above everything else and when suffering from insomnia dreams up outlandish philanthropies and then carries them out, despite protest, so that he has run up vast debts. He writes me that he has been very touched by the sight of the widow Wibrandis and the orphaned children. When he comes to Constance, if Providence has destined that the lady be Margareta, they will know it. When he goes to Augsburg I am afraid that Sabina may wrap him around her finger.[13]

Bucer got his way. Nine months after Oecolampadius' death, Wibrandis and Wolfgang Capito were married. Although, like Oecolampadius, Capito was an academically brilliant reformer, at the forefront of political and theological life, in every other way they could not have been more different. Oecolampadius was, according to Zwingli, 'a gentle and firm man'.[14] From Bucer's description Capito sounds the complete opposite. The humanist Erasmus gives a more positive description: 'A fertile mind, keen judgement, no ordinary skill in three tongues ... of such integrity, so upright a character that I never saw anything more invulnerable.'[15] We don't know what Wibrandis made of her new husband. She was probably never asked. Although his personality seems rather adolescent, he was in fact in his fifties when they married. Wibrandis was still only twenty-seven. Apart from her youth, she must have had a lot to recommend her. Capito, who had no children, took on not only his new young wife but also her four children under seven and a new mother-in-law.

Wibrandis and her family moved to Strasbourg, where Capito worked. The move was less stressful than it might have been as she was already friendly with Elisabeth Bucer and soon got to know Katharina Zell – but it must have been strange stepping into the shoes of her friend Agnes, particularly as Capito made no secret of how much he had loved his first wife. Once again Wibrandis calmly slotted into her new role. She was the perfect partner for the rash and brilliant Capito. She managed the household budget efficiently, entertained in the manner expected of a minister's wife and enabled her husband to focus on his work. She also gave birth to five more children – three girls (Agnes, Dorothea and Irene) and two boys (John Simon and Wolfgang). At the same time she had to cope with the death of her daughter Irene from her marriage to Oecolampadius. Perhaps calling her next new baby the same name was a mother's way of preserving her memory, though she would have considered herself blessed that only one of her nine children had not survived. While their marriage was not based on romance, Capito seems to have been an appreciative husband, and in Strasbourg Wibrandis had a wide and supportive network of Christian friends. Her daughter Wibrandis, aged seventeen, was married to a local brass worker. Life was good once more.

Wibrandis' settled and contented life was shattered by that sixteenth-century horror – the plague. In 1541 the disease struck Strasbourg. Out of a population of around 20,000, 2,500 died – including her children Eusebius, Dorothea and Wolfgang, and her husband, Capito. Hers was not the only family to suffer. Martin Bucer, Capito's colleague, had already lost eight of his thirteen children before the plague arrived. He now lost four of the remaining five and his much-loved wife, Elisabeth – only his disabled son, Nathaneal, survived.

On her death bed Elisabeth Bucer learnt of Capito's death from Katharina Zell, who had come to care for the dying woman. The day after Capito died, Elisabeth summoned Wibrandis to her bedside and begged her to marry her husband. She told Bucer her plan, who described the scene: 'With tears I listened to her, but answered nothing.'[16] Elisabeth died later that day. The whole proposal seems extraordinary to us – but Wibrandis would need a home and Bucer would need a wife, and Elisabeth thought this was the perfect solution both for her friend and for her husband. Even in an age of swift remarriage the couple had to leave a little time before the wedding for respectability's sake – but by the following spring Elisabeth got her dying wish and Wibrandis and Bucer were married. It was a practical rather than a romantic decision. Bucer wrote, 'My motives for taking this step are (1) loneliness and (2) the danger which exists if a person starts a household with someone he does not know. Further, there is the virtuous character of this widow and the love I owe the orphaned children of the man who made himself so useful to me.'[17] He knew Wibrandis would make a good minister's wife – she had an excellent track record! As Bucer summarised, 'In past years she has really proven that she is not only pure, honourable, faithful and godly, but also a diligent helper, who fruitfully made herself useful to the church and has a gift for ministry as for many years she demonstrated in her marriage to those two precious men of God Oecolampadius and Capito.'[18]

Between them, over the last few months, the couple had lost a husband, a wife and seven children. Today that sort of tragedy would seem unbearable, but despite – or perhaps because of – their bereavements, Wibrandis and Bucer simply got on with the ministry to which God had called them. The blended family consisted of Wibrandis, Aletheia (her one surviving child with Oecolampadius), Agnes, John Simon and Irene (her surviving children with Capito), her elderly mother, Bucer, his son Nathaneal, and, for a time, his father and step-mother. Wibrandis cared for the home and family, as she had in her previous marriages, and enabled her husband to work wholeheartedly for the gospel. Her help was appreciated. Bucer wrote, 'It is surely the Lord who has provided this helper in my cares and work. He provides so that I may obey and serve him, just as she, without a doubt, will serve me with faithfulness and devotion.'[19] His only criticism was that she was too nice to him – also that she was not his beloved Elisabeth: 'There is nothing I could desire in my new wife save that she is too attentive and solicitous. She is not as free in criticism as was my first wife, and now I realise that such a liberty is not only wholesome but necessary ... I only hope I can be as kind to my new wife as she is to me. But oh, the pang for the one I have lost!'[20]

Soon Bucer was engaged again in the task of not only running a parish and leading reform in Strasbourg but also travelling to other cities to encourage reformers elsewhere. The year after their marriage he was invited to help reform the diocese of Cologne and spent a year in Bonn. While he was away, their son Martin was born, but sadly only lived a few months. Wibrandis had to cope with the birth and the death of her child alone. Elisabeth was born two years later – named after Bucer's late wife! Wibrandis got used to holding the fort when he was away. A friend wrote, 'Butzer [Bucer] is away on some business. I do not know where. His wife is having to take care of her sick mother and two sick children.'[21] When he was at home, she still did not see much of him, due to his busy schedule – but life was far more hectic, with a stream of visitors to entertain. A Protestant exile from Italy described life in the Bucer household:

For 17 days after my arrival I was entertained in Butzer's home. It is like a hostel, receiving refugees for the cause of Christ. In his family during the entire time I saw not the least occasion of offense but only ground for edification. His table is not lavish nor sparse, but marked by godly frugality ... Thanks is given to God in Christ for all. Before and after the meal a passage is read from Scripture, followed by comment. I never left the table without having learned something. Butzer is constantly occupied in preaching, administration, and pastoral care and in influencing the government. There is scarcely a day when he does not go to the town hall. He devotes his nights to study and prayer, and I have never awakened without finding him still up.[22]

Throughout this description of the family's home life Wibrandis – the one keeping everything running so efficiently – is not even mentioned!

Bucer had chosen to travel to Germany; other journeys were less voluntary. Although Archbishop Cranmer had already invited Bucer to come and help with the establishment of the Church of England, he only agreed after he was forced into exile from Strasbourg. Under the Interim Agreement[23] the city council had agreed that Roman Catholic services should be allowed in some churches. Bucer refused to agree and was expelled. He travelled to England with Fagius, another exile, while Wibrandis looked after the family at home – in an increasingly hostile Strasbourg.

Bucer was welcomed with open arms in England. After spending some time in London, where he was involved in Bible translation – and enjoyed musical evenings with Archbishop Cranmer and spent time with King Edward VI – he moved to Cambridge to take up a teaching post. He hated it! It was cold and damp, and he thought the diet was revolting – nothing but meat. His health deteriorated. He survived one winter on his own, but the following summer he wrote to Wibrandis, urging her to make plans to join him. That would not be easy as the authorities would make it as hard as possible for her to go to her husband in exile. Bucer wrote,

How I would love to have you here, but we are in the Lord's hands. If you cannot come, I wonder if a trusty brother and his wife might come and cook for us in the winter and look after the house. You know what kind of housekeeper I am. If I could have that hope I could the better spare you until the times improve, but I am in the Lord's hands … you can make the journey in eight days and during that time your absence would scarcely be noticed.

Give the impression that you expect to winter in Strasbourg. You can come down the Rhine as far as Nimwegen, then overland 12 miles. Don't let the ship's people know what it's all about ...[24]

——————————◆—◆·◆—————————

Wibrandis travelled with her daughter Agnes and essential supplies for Bucer – sausages, sugar, plums and pills as requested! Bucer was delighted to see her. He wrote, 'My wife arrived just in time: I had become completely cold but she has warmed me up again.'[25] She returned home almost immediately, leaving Agnes to care for Bucer while she prepared to move the rest of the family to England.

In her absence the Strasbourg authorities had made moves to confiscate the family property. Wibrandis was defiant. She may have been happy to play a supportive role in her many marriages, but she was no doormat! She wrote to Bucer, 'Let them come. I'm not afraid of them.' She was summoned to the ecclesiastical court – her son-in-law went instead as 'he didn't tell me about it until he was already gone because he was worried that I might let fly some angry words, as in fact I might have!' Despite her temper, she trusted the situation to God: 'Mr Kniebis has counselled me that I shouldn't worry. So I haven't. I leave it to God. He will help me. Keep your chin up.'[26]

By the time Wibrandis managed to return to England, the poor climate and diet had taken their toll. Bucer's colleague Fagius had died and he was seriously unwell himself. He expected to die soon and had already written a will, which expressed his appreciation of his wife. He insisted that the executors take account of her ministry through her last three marriages:

Already in her first and best years she had been harshly trained in the service of the church, first by the serious and hardworking Oecolampadius and then by Capito, who was also continually troubled by illness, and finally by me, where she was enormously busy taking care of all kinds of guests who stopped over at our place, while in all this she herself was frequently sick as well.[27]

Just before his death in February 1551, he added a note to the will in which he gave her permission to marry again should she wish to: 'I believe my wife would be very well able to manage without being married, but I absolutely do not want this for her, if the Lord should offer her a husband who is godly and devout and who would be willing to assist a woman who has been so much weakened by exertions, dangers and setbacks.'[28] It sounds as though Bucer understood that Wibrandis deserved a husband who would look after her for a change!

Following Bucer's death, Wibrandis showed that she was 'very well able to manage without being married'. The family was stranded in a strange country without sufficient funds to get home, so Wibrandis wrote a begging letter to Cranmer, the Archbishop of Canterbury – her husband had done so much to help the Church of England, surely his family deserved some help in return. With the financial help Cranmer provided, she eventually was able to get everybody back to Strasbourg – no mean feat given the difficulties of travel in sixteenth-century Europe.

Wibrandis was still only forty-seven years old, and given her pedigree and reputation would easily have found a fifth husband – but she chose to remain single. Her daughter Alatheia Oecolampadius was now married to Christoph Soll, who had worked as Bucer's assistant, and he was happy to serve as her male protector when needed, and knew she could be trusted to care for his family when he was away.[29] Tragically plague struck Strasbourg once again, killing Soll and removing the final reason for her to remain in the city. She moved back to her home town of Basel.

Soon after the move, her daughter Agnes Capito married a pastor in the city – the son of the mayor. Wibrandis helped care for the growing family, and no doubt enjoyed a level of independence she had never known before. She must have been delighted that Agnes' first daughter was called Wibrandis. The compliment was repeated by two other daughters. Irene Capito called a son Wibrandus, and her youngest daughter Elisabeth Bucer also called her first daughter Wibrandis in honour of her mother. She was obviously a great mum, not only to her own children but also to Nathanael Bucer, her disabled step-son, as well as her niece Margarethe Rosenblatt, whom she had adopted on the death of her parents. Just before his death, Bucer wrote to Nathanael that 'you know that Wibrandis is to you no step-mother, but a true mother indeed'.[30] She had maintained a stable and loving family unit through bereavements and upheavals that would have torn many families apart. Her daughters also must have enjoyed being part of a large family – Agnes had fourteen children and Elisabeth thirteen!

Most of her family were devoted to her – but not all! Even the best mother cannot guarantee producing perfect children. Her son John Simon Capito was a constant worry – he seems to have inherited some of his father's unpredictable personality traits. Wibrandis wrote to him while he was a student at Marburg University,

I haven't heard from you for some time, but I well know that if I had, the news would not have been comforting. You continue always to be a cross to me. If only I might live to the day when I have good

news from you. Then I would die of joy. Be thrifty,
study hard, no drinking, gaming or wenching. If
you would follow in the steps of your father, then
Grandma, the sisters, and the in-laws would lay
down their very lives for you. But if you won't
behave differently, no one will give you a heller.
If you will behave yourself properly, come home.[31]

She was spared the final anxiety when he went missing without trace three years after her death.

She was a widow for thirteen years – four years longer than her longest marriage. Although Bucer commented on her ill health and hard life, she lived to the relatively old age of sixty, and in the end it was that scourge of her family – the plague – that killed her. In 1564 almost half the total population of Basel died. A citizen described the scene:

Every day, such a multitude of men, women and
children died off that each one could no longer
be buried individually; great pits were dug and
a dozen or two buried together. It is unbelievable
how, from about midday until about 2:00 and
4:00 o'clock in the afternoon, the bodies were
carried from all the streets to the pits in the attempt
to get the dead buried.[32]

The summer months were the worst, and those that survived until the autumn must have thought they were safe – but Wibrandis died in November. At least that meant she was able to be given a decent funeral, and was laid to rest next to her second husband, Oecolampadius, in the cloisters in Basel.

Wibrandis was a wonderful wife! She did not see marriage as a place to fulfil her emotional needs or to build her self-esteem, but as a place to serve Christ and his people. Today it seems rather strange that she could be passed from husband to husband so efficiently, and that she could play her role so well almost regardless of the man she was married to – certainly our understanding of what a successful marriage looks like would be very different from hers! Wibrandis was never given roses and chocolates on Valentine's Day, but she was loved and respected by her husbands. They knew they could trust her to care for them and their children, and to be hospitable and practical. They also appreciated her solid faith and capable personality, which meant they could carry out their public ministries without distraction. Such selflessness for the cause of Christ was rare then and even rarer now. No wonder she was so sought after.

BIBLE STUDY & REFLECTION

Philippians 2:1–18

1. How did Wibrandis put verse 3 to 4 into practice during her four marriages? In particular think about her attitude to her husbands, children and guests.

2. Which aspect of Wibrandis' life would you find most challenging?

3. From a twenty-first-century perspective Wibrandis' role might seem demeaning. How can verses 6 to 11 help us to see her attitude and achievements in a different light?

4. How can this help us as we seek to serve others in sometimes unglamorous ways?

5. Why might we feel Wibrandis had every right to complain (see v. 14)?

6. How can verses 14 to 15, and the example of Wibrandis' life, challenge our attitudes and behaviour?

7. What evidence is there that Wibrandis had a strong personality and might have struggled (as we might) to 'consider others better than [herself]' (v. 3)?

8. How can verse 13 encourage us as we struggle to share this Christ-like attitude?

CHAPTER SIX

Idelette Calvin
1510–1549
A Misguided Marriage?

There is often a lot of pressure on single Christians to feel that they should be married – that somehow they are incomplete without a partner. It's tempting for those who are married to try 'helpfully' to set up unattached friends. It is often assumed that marriage is the ideal state and that singleness is second best. There were similar assumptions in the sixteenth century. For a

Protestant minister, marriage, it seems, had become the only option. Singleness brought with it hints of Roman Catholicism, with its supposedly celibate priesthood. Pastors were now expected to have a model wife and family to set an example for their congregation, and to show that they had definitively broken with Rome. The Luthers had set the bar high with their affectionate, if sometimes volatile, relationship. Zwingli's marriage to Anna brought him the stability he needed to work for the gospel. The Zells created a great ministry team. The popularity of Wibrandis as a wife – and the speed with which she was married off each time – shows what a high value the reformers placed on the importance of marriage and family life. Bucer, in particular, was always plotting to find suitable wives for his many colleagues. The problem was that in breaking away from the unbiblical practice of clerical celibacy, the reformers seemed to have been leaning towards an equally unbiblical pattern of almost compulsory clerical marriage – even the ultra-biblical John Calvin succumbed, perhaps against his better judgement.

John Calvin, or Jean Cauvin, was a Frenchman. He was born in 1509, and so was only eight when Luther published his ninety-five theses and started the drive for reform. He was not only a generation younger than the other church leaders we have looked at, he was also different in that he had never made vows of celibacy as either a priest or a monk. As a young man he had a humanist education and had trained as a lawyer. At some stage, in his early twenties, he was persuaded of the truth of the gospel – that salvation was by faith alone and by grace alone – and that the source of authority for the Christian was the Bible and not Roman Catholic teaching. In France that was a dangerous position to take. While he was studying at the Sorbonne in Paris, the university authorities decided to clamp down on Protestant teaching. He moved around various provincial cities, further from the reach of the authorities, before being forced to flee his homeland in 1534, following mass arrests and executions of known evangelicals.

He spent a year in Basel, where he wrote the first edition of his famous *Institutes of the Christian Religion*, before briefly returning to France to sort out his dead father's estate. This time when he left, he brought with him his brother Antoine and half-sister Marie, who had both also become Protestants. The plan had been to go to Strasbourg, but while they made a brief stop in Geneva, the fiery reformer Guillame Farel used all of his persuasive powers to get Calvin – the now famous writer of the *Institutes* – to work with him to bring reform to the city. Reluctantly Calvin agreed. It was the start of possibly the greatest experiment in church reform the world has ever seen – the problem was that Geneva was not that keen! Calvin was young and inexperienced; Farel was twenty years older, but hot-tempered and impatient. The two men went too far too fast, and when, only a year after Calvin arrived, they demanded that every citizen sign up to their reformed confession of faith, the people proved less than enthusiastic. Added to this was the fact that the reformers were both foreigners, whom some accused of working for the French government. Only two years after Calvin came to Geneva, he and Farel were expelled from the city.

Calvin left with his tail between his legs, convinced that he was not fit for public life. He planned to live quietly in Basel. When Bucer asked him to Strasbourg to help minister to the growing number of French Protestant refugees in the town, he initially refused. He wrote to a friend,

> *I fear above all things a re-entry into the responsibilities from which I have been delivered, considering the perplexities I had when I was enmeshed therein. For even as then I felt the calling of God which had bound me, and in which I had consolation, now, on the contrary, I am afraid of tempting him if again I take up such a burden, which I have known myself unable to bear.*[1]

Bucer wouldn't take 'no' for an answer, and eventually Calvin agreed to stay.

Calvin stayed in Strasbourg for three years. After the unpleasantness in Geneva, it was a welcome change. He was surrounded by like-minded colleagues, and was kept busy pastoring a French congregation, lecturing on the Bible, tutoring students at home and working on a new edition of the *Institutes*. His initial financial difficulties were solved when the city council agreed to pay him for his preaching, and as he took in more boarders who paid for lodging and tutorials. What more could he want? Bucer thought he knew ...

Calvin was approaching thirty, beyond the normal age of marriage, but was in no rush to find a wife. He wrote, 'I have never married, and I do not know whether I ever will. If I do, it will be in order to be freer from many daily troubles, and thus freer for the Lord. Lack of sexual continence would not be the reason I would point to for marrying. No one can charge me with that.'[2] Elsewhere he said, 'I am still not married and do not know whether I ever will be. If I take a wife it will be because, being better freed from numerous worries, I can devote myself to the Lord.'[3]

Interestingly it was only after Calvin arrived in Strasbourg that there is any mention of marriage at all in his letters to friends. Perhaps even these comments, explaining why he had not married, show that he was under some pressure to tie the knot. Bucer, at this stage married to his first wife, Elisabeth, wanted all his fellow ministers to experience the same domestic bliss as he did – and went to great lengths to matchmake. Many married Christians today can feel the same, and push single friends into relationships or make them feel second rate for being unattached. Calvin's argument is far more biblical – clearly echoing Paul's teaching in 1 Corinthians 7. Marriage is good, but he would only marry if it made his ministry more effective – or if he was unable to remain celibate. Over the next few months, however, as Bucer got to work, we can see Calvin's resolve beginning to crumble.

It is possible that his colleagues truly believed that marriage would help Calvin cope with the many ministerial and emotional pressures he had to deal with. Soon after he arrived in Strasbourg, feeling depressed about his failure in Geneva, Calvin had to cope with the death of two close friends. He was grief-stricken. He confessed, 'I am utterly exhausted by these melancholy thoughts all night long.'[4] He was devastated when a good friend from France decided to return to the Roman Catholic Church. He was stressed and struggled to keep his temper under control: 'I sinned grievously through not keeping my temper. For my mind was so filled with bile that I poured out bitterness on all sides … When I got home, I was seized with an extraordinary paroxysm and could find no relief but in tears and sighs.'[5] Perhaps a woman could help.

Calvin had only been in Strasbourg for three months when a bride had been found for him. In a long letter to Farel, in the middle of other news, and thoughts on the political and religious situation, Calvin opened his heart to his friend,

> *Would that only a single opportunity were allowed me, in a familiar and confidential way, to confide to you all my hopes and fears, and in turn to hear your mind and have your help, whereby we might be the better prepared. An excellent opportunity will occur for your repairing hither, if, as we hope, the marriage shall come to pass. We look for the bride to be here a little after Easter. But if you will make me certain that you will come, the marriage ceremony might be delayed until your arrival. We have time enough beforehand to let you know the day. First of all, then, I request of you, as an act of friendship, that you would come … For it is altogether indispensable that someone from thence be here to solemnise and ask a blessing upon the marriage. I would rather have you than anyone else.[6]*

Is there just a slight note of panic as he begs his old friend to be there for the wedding? Looking back he said he had 'voluntarily led a single life for many years'.[7]

Was he now being steamrolled down the aisle by his well-meaning colleagues? In fact nothing came of this proposed marriage – it is unclear why. Yet almost immediately there was another potential wife on the scene, this time found by Farel – perhaps in response to a letter from Calvin in which he described his very unromantic view of life: 'Remember well what I seek for in her. I am not of the insane race of those lovers who, once taken in by a woman's beauty, cherish even her faults. The only beauty that seduces me is that of a woman who is chaste, considerate, modest, economical, patient; who I can hope, finally, will be attentive to my health.'[8] This plan collapsed before the couple even met.

Now it was clear that Calvin was on the market, and the reformer was an eligible bachelor – more young women were thrust in his path. Calvin was getting used to the idea of getting married, although the next woman also didn't quite fit the bill. Once again he wrote to Farel,

> *I am so much at my ease, as to have the audacity to think of taking a wife. A certain damsel of noble rank has been proposed to me, and with a fortune above my condition. Two considerations deterred me from that connection – because she did not understand our language, and because I feared she might be too mindful of her family and education.*[9]

Her family would not be put off, even when Calvin insisted he would not have her unless she learned French. He took matters into his own hands: 'Thereupon, without further parley, I sent my brother, with a certain respectable man, to escort hither another, who, if she answers her repute, will bring a dowry large enough, without any money at all. Indeed, she is mightily commended by those who are acquainted with her.' Calvin seemed very keen on the match: 'If it come to pass, as we may certainly hope will be the case, the marriage ceremony will not be delayed beyond the tenth of March ... I make myself look very foolish if it shall so happen that my hope again falls through.'[10] In what was becoming a pattern, the wedding did indeed look as if it was going to fall through – leading the family of the 'damsel of noble rank' to petition once more for her to become the new Mrs Calvin. At the end of March 1540 Calvin wrote, 'We are as yet in a state of suspense as to the marriage, and this annoys me exceedingly, for as much as the relations of that young lady of rank are so urgent that I may take her unto myself, which, indeed, I would never think of doing, unless the Lord had altogether demented me.'[11] By June Calvin was ready to give up. He didn't want to marry the wealthy woman, and his brother's choice, with such excellent credentials, didn't turn out to be such a good catch after all: 'I have not yet found a wife, and frequently hesitate as to whether I ought any more to seek one. Claude and my brother had lately betrothed me to a demoiselle. Three days after they had returned, some things were told me which forced me to send away my brother, that he might discharge us from that obligation.'[12] Despite all his friends and family working on the case, Calvin had not found a wife.

Finally, Idelette de Bure enters the story. In June Calvin had almost resigned himself to a single life – by August he was married. After all the matchmaking, plotting and disappointments, Calvin seems to have actually fallen in love. Unlike all of the other prospective brides, he already knew Idelette, and despite Calvin's claims only to be interested in spiritual beauty, Farel observed that she was 'actually pretty'.[13] In many ways she seemed an unsuitable match. She was a widow with two young children, which was not a problem in itself – the problem was that her husband, Jean Stordeur, had been an Anabaptist[14] leader. Calvin had known the couple in Geneva, where he and Farel had tried to convince them of the error of their ways. Although they failed, Idelette and Jean eventually turned up at Calvin's church in Strasbourg, where finally, after sitting under his preaching for over a year, they became orthodox Protestant believers. Within a few months Jean was dead, killed like so many others in an outbreak of bubonic plague, and within another few months Idelette and Calvin were married. This time we have no letters between Calvin and his friends to tell us about the progress of the courtship – presumably because Idelette was a widow who lived locally, so no third parties needed to be involved. Unfortunately that means we know nothing of how or why Calvin proposed – why suddenly, after so many false starts, he decided that Idelette was 'the one'. We don't know what Idelette thought of the proposal. As a widowed mother of two young children, with a dubious theological background, she was probably just grateful for any offer of marriage.

We don't know very much either about the nine years the couple spent together after the wedding. Although Calvin wrote volumes and volumes of sermons, commentaries and letters, he wrote almost nothing about his personal life. We can get an idea about his general views on marriage and family from these theological works. He shared the accepted sixteenth-century assumption that women were inferior: 'From where come industry and all the arts and sciences? From where comes work? From where all the things that are most excellent and that we most value? It is certain that all come from men.'[15] He also expected wives to be compliant housewives and mothers. Women 'by the ordinary law of nature are born to obey ... A woman does well when she keeps house, makes her bed, sweeps, boils the pot, takes care of her children.'[16] His contemporaries, both male and female, would almost unanimously have agreed with him – feminism was a long way in the future.

Nonetheless Calvin did stress in his commentary on Ephesians 5 that it was a husband's duty to love his wife and that demands for a wife's obedience should never lead to tyranny. He even challenged those who still held that celibacy was an ideal, saying that 'the intercourse of husband and wife is a pure thing, good and holy' and that a husband and wife are 'equal in bed'!'[17]

We get a few more personal glimpses of Calvin's own marriage in his letters to his three closest friends[18] – Farel, Viret and Falais. Calvin's relationship with Idelette was not just based on chauvinism and theological obligation – he genuinely loved her. When, just a few weeks after the wedding, Calvin was seriously ill, he saw it as divine intervention to prevent them becoming too focused on earthly delights. He wrote to Farel, 'It seemed ... as if it had been so ordered on purpose that our wedlock might not be over joyous, that we might not exceed all bounds, that the Lord thus thwarted our joy by moderating it.'[19]

He may have been a loving husband, but ministry always came first for Calvin, which presented other challenges for the newly-weds. The honeymoon period was very short indeed. Calvin was away for thirty-two of the first forty-five weeks of their marriage, attending conferences and visiting and encouraging ministers in neighbouring towns. With no modern means of communication, it would have been hard to maintain the relationship. Idelette would have had to get used to playing second fiddle to her husband's ministry. The absences must have been hard for her, but at least she was safe among friends in Strasbourg while he was away – but that was not always the case.

While Calvin was travelling, in the spring of 1541, plague struck the city once again – an event that must have particularly terrified Idelette, having so recently lost her first husband to the disease. It was in this severe outbreak that so many in the families of Wibrandis Rosenblatt and Martin Bucer died. Idelette and her children escaped from the city with Calvin's brother Antoine to stay in a nearby village until the danger had passed. Calvin showed the genuine concern of a new husband for his absent wife. Again he wrote to Farel, 'Day and night my wife was constantly present in my thoughts, in need of advice, seeing that she was deprived of her husband.'[20] He continued, 'Until the letter arrived which informed me that Malherbe was out of danger, and that Charles, my brother, wife, and the others were safe, I would have been all but utterly cast down, unless, as I have already mentioned, my heart was refreshed in prayer and private meditations.'[21]

Idelette's health and safety were not the only things causing Calvin anxiety during this period. Having unceremoniously thrown Calvin out of the city,

Geneva was beginning to regret its decision. The ministers who had taken over from him and Farel had proved ineffective, and the Reformed church and moral standards had declined. As the political situation changed, Calvin's return became possible and even desirable to many – but not to Calvin. He really did not want to go back to the city that had caused him so much grief and humiliation. He wrote, 'Rather would I submit to death a hundred times than to that cross on which I had to perish daily a thousand times over.'[22] Eventually it was agreed that he would be 'loaned' to Geneva by Strasbourg for the manageable period of six months – he ended up staying for twenty-three years!

Calvin had left Geneva in disgrace – on his return he was welcomed like a hero. An escort was sent to welcome him into the city and he was given the go-ahead to implement the reforms that had previously been so controversial. As soon as he arrived, the city council agreed to send transport for Idelette, the children and their possessions so that they could set up home in Geneva. A month later the council registers mention their arrival on 15 October 1541. A substantial house was provided for them in the centre of the old town. This was large enough not only for Calvin's own family (Calvin; Idelette; her son, whose name is unknown; and her daughter, Judith)[23] but also for his brother Antoine and his wife, paying borders and several servants. The city also furnished the house for them – pretty much the only things that Calvin owned were his beloved books. The city provided three beds, a wash stand, several tables and benches, three trunks and twelve stools. It still sounds rather spartan – presumably beds were shared and servants slept on the floor. Not surprisingly Calvin wrote, 'Everyone knows how simple things are in my home.'[24] Calvin was also given an adequate salary and an annual allowance of corn and wine. It was not luxurious, but for Idelette, who had known life as the wife of a persecuted and reviled heretic, it would have been a huge improvement in lifestyle. There were also opportunities to make new friends, to replace the ones she missed in the close-knit world of Strasbourg. The rue des Chanoines, where they lived, soon also housed other pastors' families to provide a network of support.

Initially Idelette was involved in the everyday tasks of a minister's wife – providing hospitality, visiting the sick and supervising the home to allow her husband to get on with his work. A few months after arriving in Geneva she visited the dying first magistrate, Ami Porral, who encouraged her in her own ministry. Calvin described the encounter: 'On the second afternoon, when my wife arrived, he told her to be of good courage whatever might happen, that she ought to consider that she had not been rashly led hither, but brought by the wonderful counsel of God, that she also might serve in the Gospel.'[25] It sounds as though she might have been a bit reluctant – questioning whether leaving Strasbourg had been the right decision and how she would fulfil the role as the chief pastor's wife, particularly as we know that when this conversation took place she was several months pregnant.

It was certainly not going to be easy. From the start Calvin had made it clear that ministry was his priority and worked unceasingly to change the theological and moral outlook of Geneva. He preached not only on Sundays but also three times during the week. He was fully involved with the political life of the city, as well as writing commentaries for publication and letters of encouragement and advice to correspondents throughout Europe. A friend described his workload: 'I do not believe there can be found his like. For who can recount his ordinary and extraordinary labours? ... He never ceased working, day and night, in the service of the Lord, and heard most unwillingly the prayer and exhortations that his friends addressed to him every day to give himself some rest.'[26] His health suffered. He complained of gout, kidney stones, pleurisy, rheumatism, migraines and tuberculosis. It's not surprising that when he was looking for a wife, he wanted someone who would be 'attentive to my health'.

Unfortunately soon after they arrived in Geneva it was Calvin who was having to care for Idelette. Far from freeing him for ministry as he had hoped, marriage threatened to divert him from his work. In July 1542 he wrote to Farel,

> *This is my especial end and aim, to serve my generation; and for the rest, if, in my present calling, an occasional opportunity offers itself, I shall endeavour to improve it for those who come after us. I have a mind to set about writing several things, but as my wife is now in ill health, not without danger, my attention is otherwise engaged.*[27]

———————◆•◆•◆———————

Idelette had lost a baby late in pregnancy and almost died. A month later she was still very unwell. At the end of a very long letter to his friend Viret — covering theological and political issues — and almost as a postscript he thanked Viret's wife for her kindness and wrote that Idelette 'is unable to reply, except by an amanuensis, and it would be very difficult for her even to dictate a letter. The Lord has certainly inflicted a severe and bitter wound in the death of our infant son. But He is Himself a Father, and knows best what is good for His children.'[28] Even in a letter to one of his closest friends at a time of family tragedy, Calvin's priority was still his work.

Her health never really recovered. Almost all the references to Idelette in Calvin's letters refer to her being unwell. Her health was not the only distraction.

His young step-daughter Judith became ill with the plague in 1544, which caused considerable concern, even though she survived.[29] Domestic problems continued to threaten his ministry when his sister-in-law was accused of adultery. Calvin demanded strict moral standards of all Genevans – for such things to be going on under his own roof challenged his authority in the eyes of his opponents.

Opponents to Calvin's reforms would do anything to damage his reputation, and unwittingly Idelette provided them with more ammunition. Finally in 1546 she gave birth to a baby boy and Calvin asked his friend de Falais to conduct the baptism. At the service Calvin acknowledged that Idelette had not been legally married to her first husband – as Anabaptists they had refused to make vows to civil authorities. This was leapt upon by the wife of one of Calvin's main critics. A year later Calvin was still upset when he wrote to Farel, 'She has cruelly wounded me. For when at the baptism of our child James, I had admitted the truth about the fault of my wife and her former husband, she calumniously asserted among her own friends, that my wife was therefore a harlot.'[30] This memory must have been very painful as their little boy did not live long and even this fact was used against Calvin by his enemies. Years later he was accused of having no natural feelings – proved by the fact that he had no living son. Calvin wrote, 'Balduin twits me with my want of offspring.

God had given me a son. God hath taken my little boy. This he reckons up among my misdeeds, that I have no children.'[31] Marriage and family life did not seem to benefit Calvin's ministry as much as he had hoped!

After little James' death, Idelette's health declined still further and Calvin himself was frequently ill. In 1548 he wrote that Idelette was 'in bed from prolonged illness. I have been struggling these days past with pain in the head, and spasms of the stomach, to such a degree as to cause violent convulsions'.[32] When finally she was sent on a rest cure to their friends the Virets in Lausanne, Calvin worried that Idelette was a nuisance to them too: 'It is truly a source of pain to me that my wife should have been so great a burden to you.'[33] In fact the couple were happy to help their friend.

Idelette finally died in 1549, when she was around forty years old. Calvin was grief-stricken. He opened his heart to his closest friends. To Farel he wrote, 'I do what I can to keep myself from being overwhelmed with grief. My friends also leave nothing undone that may administer relief to my mental suffering.'[34] Writing to Viret he perhaps overstated the case: 'As long as she lived she was the faithful helper of my ministry. From her I never felt even the slightest hindrance.'[35] He wrote a long and moving description of Idelette's death in the letter, emphasising her faith and her concern for her children: 'When she felt her voice suddenly failing

her she said "Let us pray: Let us pray: All pray for me."'
Viret's reply is telling – despite his grief, Calvin was
now working harder than he had been able to before: 'I
have been refreshed ... by numerous messengers who
have informed me how you, with a heart so broken and
lacerated, have attended to all your duties even better
than hitherto.'[36]

There is no doubt Calvin loved Idelette and was
heartbroken when she died. He described her as the
'best companion of my life'.[37] The year after her death
Calvin dedicated his commentary on 2 Thessalonians
to Benoit Textor, the doctor who had taken such
good care of Idelette throughout her many illnesses.
However, after she died Calvin's work rate rose
enormously – he regularly preached almost twice
the number of sermons than he had before. He was
being encouraged to remarry, but during a sermon on
1 Timothy he explained why he would remain single:

> *As for me, I do not want anyone to think me*
> *very virtuous because I am not married. It would*
> *rather be a fault in me if I could serve God better*
> *in marriage than remaining as I am ... But I know*
> *my infirmity, that perhaps a woman might not be*
> *happy with me. However that may be, I abstain*
> *from marriage in order that I may be more free to*
> *serve God.*[38]

He had said something very similar ten years earlier — but had been persuaded by friends that marriage was a better option. His driven personality and his high-profile, intense ministry meant that it might well have been better for both Calvin and Idelette if he had remained single.

In a couples culture we all need to remember Paul's teaching in 1 Corinthians 7:32–3: 'I would like you to be free from concern. An unmarried man is concerned about the Lord's affairs — how he can please the Lord. But a married man is concerned about the affairs of this world — how he can please his wife.'[39] Marriage is certainly the right option for some, but not for all. We need to be careful not to idolise relationships, but to determine to serve Christ wholeheartedly in whichever state we find ourselves.

BIBLE STUDY
& REFLECTION

1 Corinthans 7:1–2, 8–9, 28b–38

1. What are the main reasons that people choose to get married nowadays?

2. What reasons does Paul give for Christians marrying (vv. 2,9,36)?

3. What reasons does Paul give for staying single (vv. 32–34)?

4. How did Calvin and Bucer's views on marriage compare to Paul's?

5. After Calvin's marriage how did Paul's warning in verses 28b and 33–5 prove correct?

6. In what ways can our relationships divert us from serving Christ?

7. In Ephesians 5:22–33 Paul gives a more positive view of marriage and how husbands and wives should relate to each other. How can both of these passages help us to get a more balanced view of marriage?

8. What should our attitude be whether we are married or single (1 Corinthians 7:35)?

9. How can Calvin's experience be a warning to us when we are tempted to idolise marriage?

EPILOGUE

I hope you have enjoyed looking into the lives of these six women from the sixteenth century. They lived a long time ago in an age of different values, expectations and challenges. 500 years later we may feel we have little in common with them and little to learn from them. That could not be further from the truth.

These women can help us as we struggle to stand for Christ in our post-Christian world. They were misunderstood and opposed just as we often are. It was as tough being a Christian then as it is today. Yet these woman managed to stand firm in the face of hostility, and therefore so, with God's help, can we. Argula von Grumbach used her position, her contacts and above all her knowledge of the Bible to stand up to both religious and political authorities at great personal cost. Wibrandis Rosenblatt suffered the consequences of her fourth husband's refusal to compromise with the Catholic authorities, when he was sent into exile and she lost her property. Nonetheless she supported and encouraged him to the end. Their example should inspire us to stand firm for Jesus at work, at home and at college – even when people we meet are negative and rude. Their example should encourage us to stand side by side with those who face far worse than negativity and rudeness as they contend for Christ in the public sphere here and around the world.

On a more everyday level we can be encouraged by how God can use even the most unlikely people in His purposes. Anna Zwingli was a pretty but unassuming woman with little influence. However, in her own quiet and gentle way she transformed her husband's life and enabled him to make a vastly significant contribution to the progress of the gospel in Europe. Wibrandis, too, with her straight-forward domesticity, was the backbone of three influential reformers. God uses all sorts of gifts, personalities and circumstances in His service. Each of us has a part to play in building up God's people – however humble that part might appear to others.

These women can also challenge us to reconsider how far we live by the values of our society and how far by the values of the Bible. Katie Luther challenged her contemporaries as she showed how God could be glorified in ordinary family life. She was prepared to go against conventional wisdom, leave the convent and live life in the light of the Bible's teaching. Katharina Zell was prepared to defy even the Protestant views of her day as she tried to exercise her gifts and serve Christ as a woman in biblically – if not culturally acceptable – ways. Surely, with better access to Scripture and 500 years of evangelical heritage, we should be able to use our knowledge of the Bible to make sure that our lives are similarly grounded in God's Word and not just conformed to twenty-first-century expectations.

We can also learn from their mistakes. Bucer was so excited that the Bible taught that ministers could marry that he thought that all his friends should get a wife. He took one part of the Bible and applied it to situations that were never intended, ignoring passages that gave a different emphasis. The results in Calvin's life were unfortunate for him and for Idelette. For a time Calvin was distracted from his ministry, while also not giving his wife the sacrificial care demanded in Ephesians 5. Like Bucer many modern Christians see marriage as universally beneficial, leading to some unwise marriages and many dissatisfied singles. We need to be aware of other areas too where an unbalanced view of Scripture might lead us and others astray.

Above all, as we seek to learn from the lives of these women, let's resolve to build our own lives on the principles that served their generation so well – Scripture alone, by faith alone, by grace alone, through Christ alone, and to God alone be the glory!

NOTES

ACKNOWLEDGEMENTS

1   Elsie McKee (Ed. and translator), *Katharina Schutz Zell: Church Mother – The Writings of a Protestant Reformer in Sixteenth-Century Germany* (Leiden NV: Koninke Lijke Brill, 1999), p. 188.

INTRODUCTION

1   These are the 'five solae', which have been said to sum up the distinctive stand points of the great reformers. In the original Latin they are: Sola Scriptura, Sola Fide, Sola Gratia, Solo Christo, Soli Deo Gloria.

KATIE LUTHER

1   Luther referred to Katharina as Käthe – which sounds the same as Katie in English.

2   Heinrich Bornkamm, *Luther in Mid-Career*, translated by E. Theodore Bachmann (London: Darton, Longman and Todd, 1983), p. 259.

3   Ibid., p. 403.

4   Ibid., p. 404.

5   Doctor Martinus is another name for Martin Luther – it was common at the time to use Latin versions of names.

6   Heinrich Bornkamm, *Luther in Mid-Career*, p. 403.

7   M.J. Spalding, *The History of the Protestant Reformation in Germany and Switzerland*, Vol. 1 (Louisville: John Murphy & Co, 1870), p. 96.

8   Ibid., p. 96.

9   Heinrich Bornkamm, *Luther in Mid-Career*, p. 259.

10 Ibid., p. 406.

11 Preserved Smith, *The Life and Letters of Martin Luther* (first published 1911; digital edition 2006).

12 Ibid.

13 Ibid.

14 William Dallmann, DD, *Katie Luther: 'She is worthy to be loved'* (Milwaukee: North-Western Publishing house, 1941; digital edition 2010).

15 Heinrich Bornkamm, *Luther in Mid-Career*, p. 407.

16 Roland H. Bainton, *Women of the Reformation in Germany and Italy* (Minneapolis: Fortress Press, 1971; digital edition 2007), loc. 146.

17 Steven E. Ozment, *When Fathers Ruled: Family Life in Reformation Europe* (The President and Fellows of Harvard College, 1983), p. 68.

18 Kirsi Stjerna, *Women of the Reformation* (Oxford: Blackwell, 2009), p. 67.

19 Steven E. Ozment, *When Fathers Ruled*, p. 70.

20 William Dallmann, DD, *Katie Luther*.

21 Ibid.

22 Ibid.

23 Ibid.

24 Steven E. Ozment, *When Fathers Ruled*, p. 69.

25 William Dallmann, DD, *Katie Luther*.

26 Ibid.

27 Ibid.

28 Barnas Sears, DD, *The Life of Luther* (Arizona: Attic Books, digital edition 2010).

29 Heinrich Bornkamm, *Luther in Mid-Career*, p. 413.

30 Ibid., p. 413.

31 Roland H. Bainton, *Women of the Reformation in Germany and Italy*, loc. 230.

32 Ibid., loc. 226.

33 William Dallmann, DD, *Katie Luther*.

34 Preserved Smith, *The Life and Letters of Martin Luther*.

35 Kirsi Stjerna, *Women of the Reformation*.

36 Ibid.

37 Ibid.

38 William Dallmann, DD, *Katie Luther*.

39 Kirsi Stjerna, *Women of the Reformation*.

40 William Dallmann, DD, *Katie Luther*.

41 *Luther's Letters to Women*, collected by Dr K. Zimmermann, translated by Mrs Malcolm (London: Chapman and Hall, 1865), pp. 156, 160.

42 It is said that it was Katie who encouraged him to respond to Erasmus' critique of predestination, resulting in the master piece 'On the bondage of the will'.

43 William Dallmann, DD, *Katie Luther*.

44 Steven E. Ozment, *When Fathers Ruled*, p. 83.

45 http://cyberhymnal.org

46 William Dallmann, DD, *Katie Luther*.

47 Ibid.

ANNA ZWINGLI

1 J.H. Merle D'Aubigné, *History of the Reformation in the Sixteenth Century*, Vol. II, translated by David Dundas Scott (Glasgow: Blackie & Son, 1853).

2 Zwingli's first name appears as Huldrych, Ulricht and Ulrich.

3 Marjorie Elizabeth Plummer, *From Priest's Whore to Pastor's Wife – Clerical Marriage and the Process of Reform in the Early German Reformation* (Farnham: Ashgate Publishing Limited, 2012), p. 172.

4 Denis R. Janz, *Reformation Reader* (Minneapolis: Fortress Press, 2008), p. 186.

5 Ibid., p. 186.

6 Steven Ozment, *The Age of Reform 1250–1550* (New Haven and London: Yale University Press, 1980), p. 387.

7 Rev. James Anderson, *Ladies of the Reformation: Germany, Switzerland, France, Italy and Spain* (Glasgow: Blackie & Son, 1887), p. 239.

8 Thomas M. Lindsay, MA, DD, *A History of the Reformation* (Eugene: Wipf and Stock, 1999), p. 38.

9 Raget Christoffel, *Zwingli: Or the Rise of the Reformation in Switzerland – A Life of the Reformer*, translated from the German by John Cochran Esq (Edinburgh: T&T Clark, 1858), p. 13.

10 Ibid., p. 123.

11 Ibid., p. 376.

12 Art. II Huldreich Zwingli's Werke, *The Biblical Repertory and Princeton Review*, Vol. XIII (M.B. Hope, Education Rooms, Princeton, 1841), p. 211.

13 Edward J. Furcha, *Women in Zwingli's World* (www.Zwingliana, 2010), p. 136.

14 Raget Christoffel, *Zwingli*, p. 378.

15 Rev. W.M.M. Blackburn, *Ulrich Zwingli, the Patriotic Reformer* (Philadelphia: Presbyterian Board of Publication, 1868), p. 112.

16 Jean Grob, *The Life of Ulric Zwingli*, translated from the German by I.K. Loos and G.F. Behringer (New York: Funk & Wagnalls, 1883).

17 Rev. James Anderson, *Ladies of the Reformation*, p. 246.

18 Raget Christoffel, *Zwingli*, p. 376.

19 Samuel Macaulay Jackson, *Huldreich Zwingli: the Reformer of German Switzerland* (New York: G.P. Putnam and Sons, 1903).

20 Raget Christoffel, *Zwingli*, p. 84.

21 Ibid., p. 85.

22 Rev. James Anderson, *Ladies of the Reformation*, p. 250.

23 Ibid., p. 256.

24 *The Correspondence of Wolfgang Capito*, edited and translated by Erika Rummel (Toronto: University of Toronto Press, 2009) p. 466.

25 Rev. James Anderson, *Ladies of the Reformation*, p. 256.

26 Ibid., p. 258–259.

27 'Zwingli: Gallery of family, friends, foes and followers', *Christian History Magazine*, Issue 4.

28 James Isaac Good, *Women of the Reformed Church* (Sunday School Board of the Reformed Church in the United States, 1901), p. 16.

ARGULA VON GRUMBACH

1 Peter Matheson (Ed.), *Argula von Grumbach – A Woman's Voice in the Reformation* (Edinburgh: T&T Clark, 1995), p. 86.

2 Ibid., p. 110.

3 Ibid., p. 85.

4 Ibid., p. 86.

5 Roland H. Bainton, *Women of the Reformation in Germany and Italy* (Minneapolis: Fortress Press, 1971; digital edition 2007).

6 Peter Matheson (Ed.), *Argula von Grumbach*, p. 119.

7 Roland H. Bainton, *Women of the Reformation in Germany and Italy*.

8 Peter Matheson (Ed.), *Argula von Grumbach*, p. 141.

9 Ibid., p. 145.

10 Roland H. Bainton, *Women of the Reformation in Germany and Italy*.

11 Kirsi Stjerna, *Women of the Reformation* (Oxford: Blackwell, 2009).

12 Peter Matheson (Ed.), *Argula von Grumbach*, p. 79.

13 Ibid., p. 75.

14 Ibid., p. 90.

15 Ibid., p. 120.

16 Ibid., p. 149.

17 Ibid., p. 126–7.

18 Jane Couchman and Ann Crabb (Eds.), *Women's Letters across Europe 1400–1700: Form and Persuasion* (Aldershot: Ashgate Publishing, 2005), p. 278.

19 Peter Matheson, *The Imaginative World of the Reformation* (Edinburgh: T&T Clark, 2000), p. 115.

20 Ibid., p. 114.

21 Ibid., p. 117.

22 Ibid., p. 117.

23 Ibid., p. 113.

24 Jane Couchman and Ann Crabb (Eds), *Women's Letters across Europe 1400–1700*, p. 292.

25 Roland H. Bainton, *Women of the Reformation in Germany and Italy*.

26 Ephesians 6:13, taken from the Holy Bible, New International Version, 1984.

KATHARINA ZELL

1 Elsie McKee (Ed. and translator), *Katharina Schutz Zell: Church Mother — The Writings of a Protestant Reformer in Sixteenth-Century Germany* (Leiden NV: Koninke Lijke Brill, 1999), p. 226.

2 Ibid., p. 226.

3 Ibid., p. 64.

4 Roland H. Bainton, *Women of the Reformation in Germany and Italy* (Minneapolis: Fortress Press, 1971), p. 55.

5 Elsie McKee (Ed. and translator), *Katharina Schutz Zell*, p. 188.

6 See Luke 10:38–42.

7 Elsie McKee (Ed. and translator), *Katharina Schutz Zell*, p. 82.

8 Roland H. Bainton, *Women of the Reformation in Germany and Italy*, p. 62.

9   Elsie McKee (Ed. and translator), *Katharina Schutz Zell*, p. 227.

10 Anabaptists were the first to practise believers' baptism, but some of their number also held extreme theological views, such as polygamy and the value of spiritual inspiration rather than biblical authority.

11 Roland H. Bainton, *Women of the Reformation in Germany and Italy*, p. 64.

12 Ibid., p. 65.

13 Timothy J. Wengert and Charles W. Brockwell, Jr (Eds), *Telling the Churches' Stories: Ecumenical Perspectives on Writing Christian History* (Grand Rapids, Michigan: Wm. B. Eerdmans, 1995), p. 90.

14 Ibid., p. 88.

15 Elsie McKee (Ed. and translator), *Katharina Schutz Zell*, p. 117.

16 The new wife was Wibrandis Rosenblatt – see the following chapter.

17 Elsie McKee (Ed. and translator), *Katharina Schutz Zell*, p. 93.

18 Ibid., p. 95.

19 Reference not found.

20 Elsie McKee (Ed. and translator), *Katharina Schutz Zell*, p. 111.

21 Roland H. Bainton, *Women of the Reformation in Germany and Italy*, p. 67.

22 Elsie McKee (Ed. and translator), *Katharina Schutz Zell*, p. 188.

23 Ibid., p. 191.

24 The Strasbourg Magistrates negotiated with the Holy Roman Emperor following defeat in the Schmalkaldic War. The Interim Agreement allowed Catholic services to be held in the city. Many of the city's reformers refused to agree to its terms and were given a short time to prepare before being sent into exile.

25 Elsie McKee (Ed. and translator), *Katharina Schutz Zell*, p. 233.

26 Ibid., p. 191.

27 Roland H. Bainton, *Women of the Reformation in Germany and Italy*, p. 67.

28 Ibid., p. 68.

29 Elsie McKee (Ed. and translator), *Katharina Schutz Zell*, p. 196.

30 Ibid., p. 132.

31 Ibid., p. 213.

WIBRANDIS ROSENBLATT

1   Wolfgang Capito, edited and translated by Erika Rummel, *The Correspondence of Wolfgang Capito 1524–1531* (Toronto: University of Toronto Press Inc., 2009), p. 268.

2   Roland H. Bainton, *Women of the Reformation in Germany and Italy* (Minneapolis: Fortress Press, 1971), p. 81.

3   Ibid., p. 82.

4   Ernst Staehelin, translated by Ed L. Miller, *Frau Wibrandis: A Woman in the Time of the Reformation* (Eugene, Oregon: Wipf & Stock, 2009) p. 16.

5   Roland H. Bainton, *Women of the Reformation in Germany and Italy*, p. 82.

6   Jeff Fisher, 'The state of research of the Basel Reformer, Johannes Oecolampadius, with a focus on the history of biblical interpretation' (Deerfield, Illinois: Research paper, Trinity Evangelical Divinity School, December 2009), p. 1.

7   Irene Backus, *Life Writing in Reformation Europe: Lives of Reformers by Friends, Disciples and Foes* (Aldershot: Ashgate Publishing, 2008), p. 56.

8   Moderate Anabaptists differed from other Protestant groups in demanding adult baptism, which in a sixteenth-century context meant rebaptising those who would have been baptised as infants, and in refusing to take oaths to secular authorities. Both beliefs demanded that the church should be visibly separate from secular society, which was seen as a threat to community cohesion. More radical Anabaptists were far less orthodox, arguing for polygamy and in some cases even more extreme practices.

9   Roland H. Bainton, *Women of the Reformation in Germany and Italy*, p. 84.

10 Ernst Staehelin, translated by Ed L. Miller, *Frau Wibrandis*, p. 28.

11 Wolfgang Capito, edited and translated by Erika Rummel, *The Correspondence of Wolfgang Capito 1524–1531*, p. 470.

12 See note 8.

13 Roland H. Bainton, *Women of the Reformation in Germany and Italy*, p. 85.

14 Jeff Fisher, 'The state of research of the Basel Reformer, Johannes Oecolampadius, with a focus on the history of biblical interpretation', p. 1.

15 Peter G. Bietenholz and Thomas Brian Deutscher (Eds), *Contemporaries of Erasmus: A Biographical Register of the Renaissance and Reformation*, Vols 1–3 (Toronto: University of Toronto Press, 1985) p. 262.

16 Ernst Staehelin, translated by Ed L. Miller, *Frau Wibrandis*, p. 31.

17 H.J. Selderhuis et al, *Marriage and Divorce in the Thought of Martin Bucer* (Kirksville, Missouri: Thomas Jefferson University Press, 1999), p. 124.

18 Ibid., p. 125.

19 Ernst Staehelin, translated by Ed L. Miller, *Frau Wibrandis*, p. 32.

20 Roland H. Bainton, *Women of the Reformation in Germany and Italy*, p. 87.

21 Ibid., p. 90.

22 Ibid., p. 88.

23 See note 24 in the chapter on Katharina Zell.

24 Roland H. Bainton, *Women of the Reformation in Germany and Italy*, p. 91.

25 H.J. Selderhuis et al, *Marriage and Divorce in the Thought of Martin Bucer*, p. 127.

26 Ernst Staehelin, translated by Ed L. Miller, *Frau Wibrandis*, p. 44.

27 H.J. Selderhuis et al, *Marriage and Divorce in the Thought of Martin Bucer*, p. 126.

28 Ibid., p. 127.

29 Soll was the Strasbourg delegate at the Council of Trent – the Roman Catholic initiative to reform the church. Not surprisingly he returned despondent as his views had not been listened to.

30 Roland H. Bainton, *Women of the Reformation in Germany and Italy*, p. 90.

31 Ibid., p. 93.

32 Ernst Staehelin, translated by Ed L. Miller, *Frau Wibrandis*, p. 53.

IDELETTE CALVIN

1 François Wendel, translated by Philip Maret, *Calvin: The Origins and Development of His Religious Thought* (London: William Collins Sons & Co, 1963), p. 57.

2 F. Bruce Gordon, *Calvin* (New Haven, CT: Yale University Press, 2009), p. 87.

3   Bernard Cottret, *Calvin, a Biography* (Grand Rapids, Michigan: Wm B. Eerdmans, 2000), p. 140.

4   T.H.L. Parker, *John Calvin* (Tring: Lion Publishing, 1987), p. 84.

5   Ibid., p. 86.

6   Dr Jules Bonnet, translated by David Constable, *Letters of John Calvin*, Vol. 1 (Edinburgh: Thames Constable and Co, 1855), p. 86.

7   Theodore Beza, translated by Francis Sibson, *The Life of John Calvin*, (Philadelphia: J. Whetham, 1836), p. 22.

8   Bernard Cottret, *Calvin, a Biography*, p. 140.

9   John Witte and Robert M. Kingdon, *Sex, Marriage and Family in John Calvin's Geneva: Volume 1, Courtship, Engagement and Marriage* (Grand Rapids, Michigan: Wm B. Eerdmans, 2005), p. 109.

10 Dr Jules Bonnet, translated by David Constable, *Letters of John Calvin*, Vol. 1, p. 149.

11 Ibid., p. 151.

12 Ibid., p. 167.

13 Bernard Cottret, *Calvin, a Biography*, p. 142.

14 See note 8 in the chapter on Wibrandis Rosenblatt.

15 William J. Bouwsma, *John Calvin: A Sixteenth-Century Portrait* (New York: Oxford University Press, 1988), p. 76.

16 Ibid., p. 76–77.

17 Ibid., p. 137–138.

18 Dr Jules Bonnet, translated by David Constable, *Letters of John Calvin*, Vol. 1, p. 180.

19 Ibid., p. 205.

20 Ibid., p. 214.

21 Ibid., p. 223.

22 T.H.L. Parker, *John Calvin*, p. 96.

23 We know little about Idelette's children. It is possible that her son was sent to stay with friends or relatives sometime after the move to Geneva. Judith was accused of adultery in 1562 long after her mother's death, which greatly embarrassed Calvin.

24 Scott M. Monetsch, *Calvin's Company of Pastors: Pastoral Care and the Emerging Reformed Church, 1536–1609* (New York: Oxford University Press, 2013), p. 114.

25 Dr Jules Bonnet, translated by David Constable, *Letters of John Calvin*, Vol. 1, p. 310.

26 T.H.L. Parker, *John Calvin*, p. 122.

27 Dr Jules Bonnet, translated by David Constable, *Letters of John Calvin*, Vol. 1, p. 315.

28 Ibid., p. 320.

29 Later Judith caused Calvin embarrassment when she was accused of adultery after her mother's death.

30 Dr Jules Bonnet, translated by David Constable, *Letters of John Calvin*, Vol. 2 (Edinburgh: Thames Constable and Co, 1857), p. 124.

31 Dr Jules Bonnet, translated by David Constable, *Letters of John Calvin*, Vol. 1, p. 320.

32 Dr Jules Bonnet, translated by David Constable, *Letters of John Calvin*, Vol. 2, p. 162.

33 Ibid., p. 154.

34 Ibid., p. 203.

35 William J. Bouwsma, *John Calvin*, p. 23.

36 Dr Jules Bonnet, translated by David Constable, *Letters of John Calvin*, Vol. 2, p. 202.

37 F. Bruce Gordon, *Calvin*, p. 159.

38 T.H.L. Parker, *John Calvin*, p. 121.

39 Taken from the Holy Bible, New International Version, 1984.

BOOKS BY
Clare Heath-Whyte

10Publishing is the publishing house of 10ofThose. It is committed to producing quality Christian resources that are biblical and accessible.

www.10ofthose.com is our online retail arm selling thousands of quality books at discounted prices.

For information contact: sales@10ofthose.com or check out our website: www.10ofthose.com